HANNAH IN
YORKSHIRE

Barry Cockcroft

HANNAH IN YORKSHIRE

J M Dent & Sons Ltd   London

First published 1973
Reprinted 1973 (twice)
Reprinted 1974

© Barry Cockcroft 1973

Made in Great Britain
for
J. M. DENT & SONS LTD
Aldine House . Albemarle Street . London
This book is set in 11 on 12pt Ehrhardt 453

ISBN 0 460 04176 2

Acknowledgements

I offer my sincere thanks to all those who feature in this book, for they made it possible; to Mostafa Hammuri, Peter Moth, Julie O'Hare and all the other members of the YTV film crew; to Brian Jeeves and Alan Harbour (who took the cover) for their photography; to Glynne Ivor Hughes for allowing me to publish his poem, 'The Lost Village of Semer' © Glynne Ivor Hughes 1973; but most of all to Hannah Hauxwell, whom I am privileged to call friend.

For Jackie, who waited

Contents

Introduction

On the night of 30th January 1973 Hannah Bayles Tallentire Hauxwell appeared out of a landscape made sepia by a weakly setting winter sun. Dragging a white cow behind her as she bent against a driving blizzard, she entered four million, six hundred thousand homes.

Hannah Hauxwell was the central figure of a Yorkshire Television programme called 'Too Long A Winter', one of the most acclaimed documentaries of the last decade. The public response to the programme—or to be more exact, the response to the life and personality of Hannah—was phenomenal. The switchboards of Yorkshire Television in Leeds, London, Hull and Sheffield were jammed for two days. The switchboards of all the other ITV companies transmitting the programme were also swamped. Three months after transmission national and regional newspapers were still running major features about Hannah, and mail was still pouring in for her. The programme won the Pye Award as the Best Regional Programme of the Year. Even those who didn't see the programme were swept along by the emotion. Hannah Hauxwell touched the heart of the nation.

This book is a continuation and an extension of Hannah's story. It tells of Hannah's childhood and traces the development of her extraordinary life to the present day. It also tells of some of her neighbours, past and present, who have spent their lives in the harsh beauty of Yorkshire's high Pennines and remote dales.

Low Birk Hatt Farm

Hannah
Bayles
Tallentire
Hauxwell

You could pass through Baldersdale a thousand times and never catch a glimpse of Hannah Hauxwell. Her home is set by a lonely stretch of the Pennine Way and only once a month does she follow the path of the tired, straggling hikers up the fields one and a half miles to the road at the top of the dale. Her brief contact with the world outside Low Birk Hatt Farm, where life has not changed for many generations, occurs when she lifts a cardboard carton perched on the dry-stone wall by the road. It is left there each month, and has been for years, by the grocer at Cotherstone, one of the attractive villages dotted along the road through Teesdale as it leaves Barnard Castle and winds up to County Durham.

Hannah's monthly food bill with the grocer has crept up to just over £5 these days. She has had to 'put the brake on' (one of her favourite expressions). It allows only for butter, eggs, sugar, lard, margarine, onions, tomatoes, bread, one tin of Spam and a large lump of cheese to give her the protein the doctor has warned she must have. That is not much, by any standards. But it is all she can afford on her income, which can amount to £280 a year if things go well. A little over £5 a week, and there are expenses to come out of that.

When she arrives back home with the groceries there is rarely time for Hannah to sit down and get her breath back. The calf, Septimus, always needs her and it is usually time to milk Her Ladyship, her beloved white cow. This means a chase round the pasture with a pail and three-legged stool, and feeding Septimus involves a journey with a bucket down to her only source of water, the stream which flows fifty yards from her front door and which she shares with the cattle of the surrounding pasture. Low Birk Hatt has never had

running water or electricity. It is so isolated that in winter Hannah frequently goes for more than ten days without seeing another human being. She has no man and all her close relatives are dead.

At the age of forty-six she has a gleaming halo of pensioner's white hair which sprays around a face so smooth, creamy and clear that it could be a child's. Her thin, sinewy body is clothed with intricate and seemingly never-ending layers of well-laundered rags. She speaks with a slow and touching courtesy which belongs to another age. She is probably the most vulnerable and materially deprived person in the British Isles. She is probably the most content.

Hannah Hauxwell's life of serene deprivation seems to have been ordained. It reaches back to the time she was born in 1927. Life was relentlessly hard for the ordinary folk in the Yorkshire Dales when Hannah was a child. Mechanization in the shape of tractors, harvesters and hay mowers had scarcely touched this land which traditionally accepts new technology a decade or more after most farming communities. So the work on Low Birk Hatt Farm, Baldersdale, was accomplished by sweat. Long, lonely hours and sweat.

For Hannah nothing has changed since her childhood. Indeed the Hauxwells have borne this burden with an equanimity which reaches back for generations. They were always raised to a life of constant physical hardship and expected nothing else. But there was a new harshness in the lifestyle of the Hauxwells during the childhood of Hannah. The country was on the rack of the Depression, and the working class had faced up to the last famine it was prepared to tolerate. The men of Jarrow had been on the march, a file of gaunt faces which passed silently by, just fifteen miles from the fields where Hannah's father scythed the long grass and twice a day milked his cows by hand. William Bayles Hauxwell, fighting his eighty sparse acres, knew little of this drama taking place just over the hills. Dales' farmers never did have much time to spare for affairs outside their own self-contained environment. Forty years ago the boundaries of their world were limited on the one side by the markets where they bought and sold their animals, and on the other by the heights of the

Hannah, aged six, with her mother

common grazing land where their sheep scratched a living. This insular attitude is emphasised in Balders-dale because it is a closed dale. The road just peters out on the moors at its head, and the only non-residents who travel it regularly are the men who tend the reservoirs which stretch past Low Birk Hatt.

Hannah's first memories of her father go back to happier times when he would bring back small presents for his only child whenever he visited Barnard Castle, twelve miles down the narrow lanes of Teesdale. 'He never forgot to bring me something back—usually buns from a shop called Guy's. But the treats stopped when the hard times came. I don't know how he managed, the prices were so bad.'

Most farmers in the dales go to market less than a dozen times a year, to sell their fatstock or buy new blood for their herds and flocks at those atmospheric, corrugated iron and concrete auction rings where the weekly rituals of rural business life are conducted to this day. When they do, it is a life and death matter. Even now a bad day at market can prejudice the life and plans of a family for half a year. For a long spell during the thirties every market day was bad.

The Hauxwells had an extra burden. Most farming families care for one, or perhaps two, of their old folk. But William and Lydia Hauxwell shared the dwindling comfort of their farm with four ageing relatives—William's parents and two elderly uncles. The farm-

James and Elizabeth Hauxwell

5

house which stands on the lip of Hury reservoir is an empty and echoing place today, now that only Hannah is left, but forty years ago it was full to the brim. Seven mouths to feed, money scarcer than it had ever been and only one able-bodied man. It is not difficult to understand why Hannah's mother and father decided not to add any more children to their family, but this meant that Hannah was deprived of the companionship of brothers and sisters. As a child, Hannah may not have gone hungry like her contemporaries in the slum terraces of the cities, since farms always have eggs and the odd hen which has outlived its usefulness, but the city children at least had the comfort of playmates and games which could help them to forget their environment.

For a time Hannah did have one small friend at the next farm down the valley, which today stands empty and crumbling like so many others in the more remote dales, where communications are poor and the land only good for grazing.

'Yes, I had Derek for a playmate when I was very young. Derek Brown from Blackton, just a little way across the valley. His mother was my father's cousin and he used to come for "Hannah girl" as he called me, so that he could walk with me to school. But he and his family left quite soon, before I was ten, and there was never anyone else.

'Those days were quite miserable because Father was doing so badly at market, just like everyone else. He used to come home depressed because he had paid a high price for the farm—£1,600—and the mortgage payments were very heavy. I once saw some of the papers he left behind with the details of his income and expenditure, and I just don't know how he managed.

'I was too young to understand properly what was going on at the time. Anyway I was busy playing around in the fields with the animals and helping to feed them. I remember we had a grand little horse called Dick—a faithful, honest horse who I used to ride occasionally. I liked it best when he used to drag a sledge like a big strong gate and I was allowed to ride on it. We had dogs too, but I wasn't allowed to play with them because they were working dogs. Except one, an old English

Hannah at ten

6

sheepdog called Roy. He used to have fits so it didn't matter me playing with him. I think I used to spoil him. As for toys, I didn't have many but that's understandable. I do recall a little rabbit someone gave me. It wasn't made in the lovely materials you have now but it was nice and soft. Now, I treasured that but it vanished rather strangely around the time that little Derek left. I'm not making any accusations but I always wondered!'

As Hannah played innocently in the farmyard, a real tragedy was developing in the Hauxwell household. Her father became ill with pernicious anaemia and the doctor announced that he would never again be a completely fit man. He was told to take care of himself and to reduce his workload, but of course he didn't—he couldn't. There was quite a sleeping problem in the house which only had three bedrooms. One uncle had to bed down in the space under the stairs, and Hannah slept in the same bed as her mother and father.

'It was a big blue bed and we all three used to sleep in that. But I remember one morning when I woke up and realised that something was different. I was in another bed in the room, all by myself and wrapped up in a soft green eiderdown. Then I saw something I'll never forget. I can picture it now. The door was open and the undertaker, all dressed in black, was standing there at the top of the stairs. You see, my father had died during the night and they'd moved me. It seems he'd been taken ill with pneumonia and he just died. He was only thirty-seven.

'I don't recall the funeral—they kept me away from that. A Miss Leach, an old friend of the family, came to look after me the day they buried him at Romaldkirk. I didn't get to know my father well because I was too young when he was alive, but I think he must have been a grand man. One of my regrets is that I don't have a photograph of him as an adult. Mother wanted one taken when they got married but he said he wouldn't bother. It cost money. But I do know that Father had many plans for us had he lived.'

Hannah's mother was left a widow with a child, a mortgaged farm and four old people to care for. This desperate situation was relieved by the arrival of

William Hauxwell as a young man. Hannah's only photograph of her father

Hannah's uncle, who was glad to come and manage the farm since the living on his own had become even more precarious than that at Low Birk Hatt. Hannah found the new member of the family a difficult person because he had marital problems and was subject to fits of depression. Unfortunately she could draw little comfort from her schooldays.

'No, I didn't like school at all. I didn't regret leaving when I was fourteen and never have to this day. I liked the under-teacher, Miss Walker, very much and I cried when she left, which was quite a bit before the war. The head teacher was a kind woman in her way and she would buy apples, oranges and sweets for us out of her own pocket at times like Whitsuntide and Christmas. But she and I just didn't get on. It's not that I was a naughty girl, I was just very shy and maybe not the quickest to pick things up. Anything I could manage I did, such as reading or spelling, but arithmetic—well! She was the sort of person, you know, who had her favourites and I wasn't the only one to become at variance with her. I always remember one day she was being cross with one of the less fortunates, and comparing him with a boy called Maurice who was a favourite. She snapped "Yes! Maurice has a *mother*," as though the other poor boy was like the character in *Uncle Tom's Cabin* who wasn't born, he just growed and hadn't had a mother. I don't think really those were my happiest days.'

Lydia, Hannah's mother, as a young girl

Hannah's relationship with her mother was the one warm, complete and stable bond of her life. Lydia Sayer Hauxwell brought into Low Birk Hatt, accomplishments which were uncommon, to say the least, in the bleak and basic life of Baldersdale. Her education and upbringing had embraced music and literature. She was a talented musician and her dowry included a small, foot-powered organ which still stands in the kitchen of Low Birk Hatt, and is played occasionally by Hannah who inherited her mother's love of music.

'Mother's mother was a lady who, I think, was born in good circumstances and brought up at the Manor House at Bowes. The family owned hotels in the area, and Mother had acquired tastes and traits through them. I remember she used to make up satin dresses for her sisters and she had received a share of good jewellery. Mother was so wonderful. I'm sorry to say I'll never be the woman she was. I don't even look like her. She was little and plump and she would sing and play the organ—and laugh. You know, when one is young one doesn't think, but in these later years I've thought a lot and come to understand just what a wonderful person she was, that having her life she could still laugh. She had to go out and work on the farm and, at the same time, nurse the elderly people who were all poorly in turn. The last to go was Grandma Elizabeth who died in 1940. We raised sheep and cattle and we all had our jobs, particularly at haymaking and sheep-shearing time. I was never much good at sheep shearing.

'Mother and I had such a lot of happiness together and I do wish we had enjoyed better circumstances. But she used to keep everyone's spirits up. We were very close. I used to hear girls at school saying that they wouldn't or couldn't tell their mothers various things, but there was nothing I couldn't and didn't tell her. We shared everything—the beauty of the countryside, the books and the music.'

The other influence in Hannah's childhood was her grandfather, James Hauxwell. He had arrived in Baldersdale one day towards the end of the nineteenth century. A dashing figure with a shovel in his hand and a poem or recitation for any occasion on his lips, James Hauxwell stood out among the navvies digging the long and winding Hury Reservoir, which banks up to the front garden of Low Birk Hatt. His home was 'up country', at a farm called Swinelayers in Manfield, between Piercebridge and Darlington, but he was a travelled man and had served with the army in India. He could quote from Kipling and other popular Victorian authors, a social attribute which gave him a decided advantage when he came to court Grandma, herself a well-read young lady. They had one other thing in common—the memory of genteel backgrounds. James's father was reputed to have been cheated out of his inheritance by an elder brother when their wealthy father died.

The memory of her grandfather still makes Hannah laugh. 'I think maybe he was a harum scarum,' she says

9

delightedly. 'I suppose drink was his fault, to a fault. But oh, how he could recite. Listening to Granda' reciting as he sat in his chair by the fire, is one of the things I remember best from my childhood. He could quote from *Bell's Elocutionist :* "Balshazzar's Feast" and the "Arab's Farewell to his Steed" and many more. It was lovely.'

Apart from Grandad James, the elder Hauxwells did not have much time to spend amusing Hannah, but when she grew old enough to wander further afield she spent a lot of time with a happy and warmhearted family at Clove Lodge, a farm perched on a hill on the other side of the reservoir. There was still no child of Hannah's age for her to play with, but she was made welcome.

'There was Mr and Mrs Atkinson and their son Douglas, who was ten years older than me, and Mrs Atkinson's two sisters, the Misses Elizabeth and Annabella Hind. After my father died I generally used to go to them for Christmas, and stop a few days.

'I can still remember the Christmases at home before Father died. I used to hang up my stocking and there would be an apple, an orange, a few sweets and nuts, a bit of coal and an onion popped inside. Once I got a dolly, but that was a special Christmas. They made quite a thing of Christmas at Clove Lodge and I loved it. They used to get a juniper tree from the hillside and put it in the middle of an old cart-wheel and we'd all gather round and decorate it with tinsel and things. There was always a present for me. I remember Mrs Atkinson gave me a brush and comb one year, and when I arrived another year Miss Elizabeth was just finishing off a little black and brown apron for me. Then they would light the fire in the east room and there would be a chicken and a plum pudding on the table. They were so kind and always encouraging me to come and visit. The only time I ever played cards and dominoes was when I stayed with them. I used to sleep on their sofa, by the window. Mind you, they had their problems because Miss Annabella took fits and I used to help look after her sometimes.

'Christmas at Clove Lodge was always something to look forward to. In later years when I was a teenager

Building Hury Reservoir immediately below Low Birk Hatt Farm. James Hauxwell is believed to be the man at the far left of the lower picture

living with Mother and Uncle, we never had what most people would call a proper Christmas. Mother and I would always go to chapel of course, and sometimes we would have a chicken. Otherwise it was just a normal day with no exchanging of presents or anything like that.'

Chapel was a strong influence in Baldersdale at that time. Today Hannah's personal library reflects the devout attitudes of the elder Hauxwells and consists largely of Bibles—sixteen at the last count—and books on theology. The Sundays of Hannah's young life were devoted to worship, and her spiritual values remain unchanged although she seldom has the opportunity of attending services these days.

'Actually we were mixed up with both church and chapel. I used to go to the church Sunday school and then to the church service afterwards. Mother and Grandma used to come to the church service and then we'd all go on to the Methodist chapel in the evening. Grandma was church and Mother was chapel, you see, so we patronised both. But I was baptised into the church.

Hannah as a young woman

'It was through the Sunday school that I managed to get out of the dale a bit. We used to go on coach trips to places like Redcar, Morecambe and the Lakes. The longest trip we ever had was to Loch Lomond. The coach picked us up at the top of the road at six o'clock in the morning and brought us back in the small hours. That's still the farthest I've ever been away from home.'

As she grew into womanhood, Hannah was expected to take a full share in the work of the farm. Although the war had given farm prices a much-needed boost, money was still not plentiful. Uncle had to be paid a good wage since he was managing the farm and supporting his wife and family, from whom he was parted. He was also hot-tempered.

'I'm afraid I did have some unpleasantness with Uncle. You see I've never been too quick at things—in fact it takes me a long time to do anything—and he would become impatient. There were bad patches. I understand now it was because he had these other stresses. His wife used to come sometimes to see him and that was never a very happy time. But he could be a jolly man sometimes and I was rather fond of him and did my best to please him. I used to help with the hay-making, following the mower round because the cutter-board dragged the grass instead of letting it lie in swathes. It was often my job to catch the horses and bring in manure and hay with the cart. Those horses were a handful and once I sprained my wrist rather badly trying to control them.

'But through all these times my mother was wonder-ful and I wished we could go away and live quietly together, without all the worries. We did own an old derelict house on a little piece of land farther down along Hury reservoir. I understand Father was planning to repair it one day, but we were never able to do anything about it and once had to sell some of the land to help things along. Mother was everything to me and even when she was in good health I'd wake up in the night and worry about what I would do without her. It was an awful time when she did become poorly. One summer she went to the doctor who sent her to hospital for X-rays, but they didn't seem to be able to help. At the back end of the year we had that dreadful Asian 'flu epidemic and we all caught it, only Mother never really picked up. She was just so weak and it got worse and worse, and then I got this feeling . . . .

'I used to cry during the night and during the day when she couldn't see me. But I did stop myself when I had to go upstairs to take her food and the things that she needed. I thought it was something I'd never be able to hide, but I managed. Both Uncle and I became very worried and I remember him coming to me one night after he'd been to see her and saying "By——she looks far worse than I ever thought she was." Then one Tuesday when I was out working she developed a bad pain, so I went up to one of the neighbours who had a telephone and they rang the doctor. An ambulance was sent and she became worse and worse as we were getting her ready. She died on the way to hospital. One has never ceased to miss her.'

It is fifteen years since her mother's death but Hannah still feels the pain as though it were yesterday. She cannot hide the tears and cannot even speak about the funeral. Lydia Hauxwell, the happy little plump

Lydia Hauxwell

13

woman who could still laugh despite the crushing blows dealt out by fate, was buried alongside the young husband she lost almost a quarter of a century before.

Poor, miserable Hannah now had no one to turn to for comfort. Her uncle had always been preoccupied with his own worries and his health also began to fail.

'I had quite a time with him. Mother was a good patient, of course, but I'm afraid that he wasn't. He wanted attention all the time and I had the farm to look after. They said he had rheumatism but I realised that it was more than that because he worsened rapidly. He was so bad that I even had to go and get a neighbour to help me get him up. Then the doctor said he'd better go into hospital in Barnard Castle. I was sorry in a way but he wasn't happy with the attention I could give him. I'm afraid he died there. I don't know now whether I should have stuck it out with him but the doctor insisted that he ought to go into hospital. I was really very fond of him, you know.'

And so Hannah found herself totally alone. She had little knowledge of the outside world and was not in any way equipped to go out and meet it on equal terms. Just once a year she has to make a business visit to the pleasant little market-town of Barnard Castle. The event always unsettles her for days. But otherwise she rarely leaves her dale—in fact rarely leaves Low Birk Hatt, except for those monthly trips to the wall by the road for her groceries. It would be a desolate life for most people but Hannah is radiantly content.

'You see, I can't see myself anywhere else or in any other position. I'm so attached to the homestead because only our family has lived in this house since it was built.

'One is free, and the lovely countryside has a strong appeal for me. It has such continuity and it'll be here for a long time yet, unless man gets too clever for himself and blows it all up. When I've been on my favourite walk down by the side of the reservoir, I've often stopped to think. I've looked around and said to myself "Well, if I haven't got money in my pocket that's one thing nobody can rob me of. It's mine . . . mine for the taking." You see, I'm not cut out to be in any other place. I have no ability, I'm not even a good

A love-hate relationship

farmer because you can't be on a shoestring. Anyway I couldn't manage to farm what I call properly, doing the haymaking and looking after a great lot of cattle. The few I keep are about what I can cope with. I have rather a love-hate relationship with them as it is, but I must say I'm very attached to my old white cow—Her Ladyship I call her—and the calf, Septimus.

'When Uncle died I decided to sell all the cattle because I was unable to care for them. Mr Tom Addison, the auctioneer, was very good and a few neighbours came to help get things ready. But it wasn't a happy day and I never went outside. I was left with about twenty bullocks and some good stirks but I was very unlucky with the prices and there was only about £500 to come back at the end of it all. Apparently the market for cattle wasn't good at the time, and I was told later that if I'd waited for another month I would have made another £4 or £5 a head. It was a bad do, and it sort of put a damper on everything.

'I've never been a business woman and I don't like handling money. I generally rear a beast to go to market once a year. Little Septimus will be the next but my friend Mr Anderson of Middleton-in-Teesdale takes it to auction for me. I wouldn't be a ha'porth of use at market with all those men—well, some of them are rough.'

Middleton-in-Teesdale auction mart is certainly no place for a maiden-lady with Hannah's sensitivities. When her beast is carried off she waits nervously at home for the result because although the auctioneer only takes about two and half minutes to dispose of the animal, it is a vital time for Hannah and yields more than a third of her astonishingly low income.

'It varies a little, of course, but I have to manage on around £280 a year. The last beast I sold, he made £108 but there were expenses to come out of that—transport and so forth. I also take a few cattle in for neighbouring farms. I look after them and graze them on my land, which brings in somewhere around £160. On top of all that I get a subsidy of around £23 for Her Ladyship and another of £10 or £11 for the calf. Out of that I have to buy the meal—that's a fairly big thing—and pay a man to do the hay-timing. Coal is rather an expensive item—over £30 a year, but I like a fire. It's one thing I've never economised on because a good fire is essential here. But it's necessary to economise on most items. I have a system of keeping expenditure down to the very bare necessities. In some respects I would say that I can't even afford some necessities so I keep it down to the bare essentials. I put the brake on and keep it on—it's the only way.'

Hannah may not have much of a farm in terms of stock and produce but she works it completely alone, and with her bare hands. She does not even own a wheelbarrow.

'I suppose I do have to be the farmer and the farmer's wife. But I've gone outside and roughed about ever since I was twelve. I've even carried sacks of coal on my back from the top road when I've been cut off by a snow storm. There are quite a few jobs I find hard to do, though, like repairing gaps in the dry-stone walls. I can manage the smaller stones all right but I often come across great big stones which I can't lift. The property, of course, is quite a headache because it's always in need of repairs, but I just carry on and do my best.

'Winter brings all sorts of problems. I have to get all my water from the stream and when it freezes I have to take a pick to it and melt the ice in the house. When

there's a long spell of dry weather the stream dries up
so I have to go and look for water somewhere else.
Having a bath is a bit of a problem. I boil the kettle on
the Calor gas stove two or three times and I do my best
to have my bath in a cowpail by the fire. It's not a fast
job. If I admitted the truth, I would say I don't have a
bath as often as I ought but I do like one if a friend is
going to call.

'Sometimes I feel I've missed a patch out of life,
missed being a woman you might say. I've never
bothered with lipstick and powder but I do like clothes.
I know I live in these old rags but I do that because the

cattle are no respectors of clothes. My best clothes are
nothing special, of course, and I only wear them on the
few occasions I go out. I have a nice blue dress someone
very kindly gave me. But I'm not a glamour girl, I don't
think, and I haven't much money to spare for buying
clothes. The last new dress I bought was a black one,

when my mother died. But friends have been kind in giving me clothes and I don't really want for them.'

Hannah's isolation and gentle introversion meant that she didn't meet many eligible young men. Much of her young womanhood was spent in the company of older people, but she has thought about marriage.

'Yes, of course, one does think. But it takes two to have an opinion of that kind—you can't just walk into a shop and say "I want a husband". When I was younger there were people I liked but there was no one really special in that line. I suppose I'm very much like the spinster lady who went to her clergyman and complained about the lack of a husband. He told her she must leave it in the Lord's hands, to which she replied "That's all very well, but up to now the Lord's made badly out!" Marriage is a wonderful thing if one is privileged to meet the right person and it turns out well. But it must be one of the worst things in the world to have to share a home and a life with someone that you become utterly at variance with.'

The loneliness and the unremitting harshness of Hannah's life, aggravated by her sparse diet, brought her to a low ebb when she was forty.

'I think I got rather down in myself. I'd been going to see the doctor for quite a while and he thought I wasn't improving very much, so he suggested I went to hospital. A neighbour very kindly agreed to look after my animals and I stayed there for eight weeks. It was the first and only occasion I've spent any length of time away from Low Birk Hatt. I was very happy there. I went a stranger and came away with one or two friends. I saw television for the first time and found it very interesting. Of course there was nothing seriously wrong with me. I'm afraid I took it rather badly when I came back. I gradually got used to the same thing again but oh, it wasn't the same when I came home at first. It seemed very quiet, and no one to talk to.'

There is a real risk that Hannah may fall ill again one day and be unable to call for help. She would have to wait for the postman to find her, or some neighbour to notice that her oil lamp had not been lit for some time. Hannah says 'It's a chance I'll just have to take.'

20   When she has time to relax Hannah likes to read and

listen to her battery radio, which was given to her by one of a small but devoted network of friends, nearly all of whom live at least 100 miles away from Baldersdale. They met Hannah as they rambled along the Pennine Way and were moved by her nun-like tranquillity and happy acceptance of her spartan life. They write and send her birthday cards and books. Unfortunately, long hours of reading by a flickering oil lamp have affected Hannah's eyesight and she has to ration this pleasure.

'The radio is a great friend of mine. I like to hear the man saying "This is the World at One" and I do enjoy "The Archers". The other night I had a real treat. I listened to "Grand Hotel", the Salvation Army Singers, the "Hebrew Slaves Chorus" and Elizabeth Schwarz-kopf singing "Don't be Cross". It was really grand, and all of a slap on the same night.

'Probably my favourite book is *Little Women*. A dear little lady across the dale sent it to me many years ago. It was the first book I ever read. There are lots of books I'd like to read but I have to be careful with my eyes these days. They ache so much. Poetry about the dales I also like very much. We had poets in Teesdale, you know—Richard Watson and William Langstaff. I particularly like some lines from Mr Langstaff, who wrote:

Long, silent hills,
Clear, singing streams.
Among them, we're close to God.

'Those lines appeal to me very much because well—they're my life. That's the picture I see every day, and never tire of it. From my window one can see the hills and the trees, and then there's Hunder Beck which runs down by the side of the house. On still summer nights it sings songs to me.'

There is something inspirational about Hannah which affects everyone who meets her. She is really of another age and another world, with a quite different set of values. Her spiritual repose, infinite trust and tranquil, uncomplaining acceptance of a way of life which is unacceptable by modern standards make her a unique person. This quality is so powerful that it does not diminish when processed by the media and projected from a television screen.

Hannah realises that her enclosed world is really incompatible with the one we know (the one which she dislikes and distrusts) and that advancing years and ill health will finally force her away from her beloved home in a hidden corner of a half-forgotten dale. There has been nothing in her life up to now to prepare her for

22

such a change. It will be like hauling someone out of the middle of the nineteenth century.

'I don't know what's the best to do. I like the house and I'd like to keep it—it's home. I think I must be a Wilkins Micawber; I'm waiting for something to turn up, maybe. Honestly, in my own mind I don't know what to do. The time will come when ill health— rheumatism maybe—or circumstances will make me consider changing my life.

'But I love it here, so the old house and me, we'll stay together for as long as we can.'

Since her appearance on television, Hannah has a new network of friends she has never seen. Hundreds of letters and scores of parcels arrived at Yorkshire Television's studios in Leeds, and many more turned up at Low Birk Hatt, on the back of a faintly astonished postman who sometimes doesn't have to call for weeks. To their credit, the G.P.O. managed to cope with addresses like 'Hannah Hauxwell, Somewhere in the High Pennines, near Teesdale', and 'Hannah Hauxwell, Star of ITV Programme "Too Long a Winter", near Barnard Castle'. For weeks after transmission, the lanes of Baldersdale were full of people trying to find her. Only a few got through to Low Birk Hatt, which is well defended by fields on one side of Baldersdale and by rough, gated tracks on the other. Two old ladies from Harrogate did struggle over the fields with a pound of sugar. Many of the letters contained a £1 note with the message that Hannah must not consider it charity; the writers felt they owed something to Hannah because she had made them reconsider their own lives and attitudes. She had given them a glimpse of values and virtues long since extinct in our way of life, but which are still lovingly preserved at Low Birk Hatt.

Three months after the programme, letters, parcels and money were still coming in steadily. Over £250—almost a year's income—has gone into Hannah's bank account; the food parcels will enrich that meagre diet for many months, and she has a wardrobe full of extra clothes. People have written poems for and about her, proposals of marriage have been made to her (and rejected in wide-eyed amazement), people have begged her to stay with them or asked to spend their holiday working at Low Birk Hatt. A local county police chief offered a task force of police cadets to do some essential work on the farm. One man wanted to buy the farm and allow her to live in it rent-free for life.

For a few days Hannah was quite overwhelmed by it all. She wanted the money sent back or given to charity. A team was formed among the television production unit to go out to Hannah again and help her deal with the situation. They are still making regular visits. Hannah was persuaded to accept the money; the letters were answered on her behalf; the money banked; a visit to the opticians for new glasses organised and extra lighting provided.

The ecology of Low Birk Hatt has not been affected. Hannah greatly enjoyed the making of the film (she even had a joyful flight in the YTV helicopter), rode the tidal wave of reaction with equanimity and has now settled back to living her normal life around the farm and its animals.

'And this winter, when I go to my bed, I'll be able to hug all these lovely memories to me.'

The Bainbridges of Birkdale

In early November 1972 a well-worn tractor, dragging an overladen trailer, nosed its way over a wild peat moor to start round two of a bitter romance.

At the wheel sat Brian Bainbridge, a forty-eight-year-old, farmer and sometime miner. Perched on a wheel-arch and clearly too happy to mind the discomfort, was his wife Mary, a thin, spare woman of forty-three. Swaying along behind was a large part of their furniture. Cane chair legs were silhouetted against a sky full of pewter menace, and on top of the chairs sat an elderly black and white border collie called Fred. The thin east wind whipped a steady drizzle into their faces and they appeared to be heading for nowhere. Ahead of them stretched as vast and sullen a landscape as you could ever wish to see in north Yorkshire, the Sahara of

England. The moor rolled away on all sides to a height of 2,000 feet, sliced by a fast-running beck which occasionally dropped spectacularly into rock gorges fifty feet deep. Apart from a few sheep, the Bainbridges were totally alone in this forbidding place and for mile after mile there appeared to be no signs of human habitation.

Yet the Bainbridges were going home. Home to Birkdale, a place they had loved and hated for seventeen years. Birkdale Farm lies hidden in a fold of land where the counties of Yorkshire, Durham and Westmorland meet by a swollen stream called Maizebeck. The farmhouse was built of local stone around the fifteenth century to house miners who burrowed for pyrites in the surrounding hills. It stands only about four miles— as the curlew flies—from Hannah Hauxwell's farm in Baldersdale.

Four years before, Birkdale had cast out the Bainbridges. A savage winter had annihilated their flock of sheep, and Mary had become pregnant again. Birkdale is situated seven difficult miles and seven gates away from what passes for a main road in those parts (the B6277 between Middleton-in-Teesdale and Alston) and thirteen miles from the nearest doctor. But in winter those seven miles might as well be seven leagues. Another winter was looming, so the Bainbridges fled.

In 1972 they were returning; responding to a call they did not fully understand but could not deny. Returning, their furniture in a haycart, to a place where Pickford's never go. At least this time Mary had the wheel-arch of a tractor to sit on and no children to worry about. Twenty-one years before, she had walked the seven miles through a blizzard, alongside a horse who was dragging their furniture on a sledge. She carried one child in her arms while another stumbled along hanging onto her skirts. Her third child was sitting on the sledge. She had no idea where Birkdale was or what it was like. When she finally arrived, exhausted, she found twelve sheep living inside her new home. She had to clean up their mess before the family could settle in, without the aid of electricity and with all water fetched by bucket from the beck. No wife ever had a grimmer start to a new life but Mary knew that this was what her husband wanted and so hid her dismay.

Brian Bainbridge had, in fact, set his heart on Birkdale when he was little more than a boy. He had been born in Weardale, the next dale, and spent his childhood roaming these heights; earning a little pocket money beating grouse for Lord Horsfield's shooting parties, and rabbiting with his ferrets and his dog. He left Forest-in-Teesdale school at the age of fourteen, with the fixed intention of becoming a sheep farmer. A tough, quiet young man dressed in cord breeches and clogs, he started work at a local farm for 7s. 6d. a week and his keep, but was wooed away after six months by the dizzy promise of £1 a week to work in a nearby winstone quarry, which supplied road-builders with stone chippings.

'I went as a blacksmith's striker, helping to put new cutting edges on the tools they used to quarry the stone. They would only stay sharp for a fortnight. I worked for an old blacksmith who was past retiring age and suffered from the shakes—most blacksmiths do, like boxers go punchdrunk. I worked the bellows and swung a 14lb. hammer when he was tempering the tools. I was a bit nervous the first week or two because I kept on hitting his knuckles, with him having the shakes. It must have hurt, but he was a strong chapel man and didn't swear. He just used to look at me and grunt. After a year I got a job in the pyrites mine at Cowgreen, close by Birkdale. We used to go a mile down in a steam-driven cage. Everything was piecework so it was good money and when I was seventeen I was given a job driving shafts through the rock. We had to make them six feet high and six feet wide, and me and another miner, Fred Beadle, were paid £3 8s. od. for every fathom (about six feet). In a good week we could drive four fathoms and have £13 8s. od. to split between us.

'When I used to come up from the mine I'd see Birkdale standing there, just over the ridge. I'd always fancied it. There was a man called Mason running it at the time.'

In 1945, at the age of 19, Brian had to stop working at Cowgreen because his body became covered in boils. The doctor put it down to lack of air and told him to quit. He went to work as a shepherd on the moors alongside Birkdale but within weeks he was called up and sent as an infantryman to Palestine. After demobilisation, Brian returned to mining and worked at several mines in the Teesdale area, digging out pyrites, wolfram and spar. He also worked at farms when the opportunity arose.

Mary came to Teesdale with the Women's Land Army. She had been born into a mining family (who, oddly enough, mined pyrites) in a village called Dunston, near Gateshead. But she was never a town girl. She was evacuated during the war to a farm near Richmond where she spent most of her girlhood, and never returned home. Then she joined the Land Army and went to work on a farm at High Force, between Birkdale and Middleton-in-Teesdale. Then Brian met her and their lightning romance shows that he was not as dour as he looked.

'We went out together in the September, and he wanted to marry me in the October, but my mother wouldn't let me and we had to wait until April. I was twenty when we married. Straight away he took me off to the highest farm in Ettersgill, above High Force. He still worked at the mine but we took the cottage there. It was three miles from the road and we had eighteen gates to open. The children came along pretty quickly— I had three babies in two years and three months—so after a year we moved to another cottage a little lower down the dale, to make things a bit easier for me.'

In 1952, after three years of marriage, the chance that Brian had hoped for since his teenage days suddenly arose. The tenancy of Birkdale came free. Brian was so eager not to miss it that he could not wait to show it to Mary before agreeing to take it.

'It didn't matter. He'd talked about this place and he'd always wanted a farm of his own—we both had, in fact—so it didn't matter where it was. I remember him saying it was a bit isolated and a bit wild but I was used to living in places like that.

'Still, we had a bit of a bad start. There was no road to Birkdale and we set off walking, with a horse dragging the furniture along on a sledge. I was carrying Tommy, who was three months old, and dragging along Jacqueline, who was two and a half. Sandra, who was just over one, had a seat on the sledge. It began to snow and the horse fell into a bog, breaking one of the shafts. When we finally arrived we discovered that someone had left the farmhouse door open and the place was full of sheep.

'For the first six months Brian worked the nightshift at Cowgreen mine and ran the farm by day, so that we could get some money to stock the place. There were already 200 sheep at Birkdale but they belonged to the landlord and we had to look after them as part of the tenancy agreement. We could keep any lambs they had but we had to leave 200 sheep behind if we gave notice. Brian did get a small monthly wage from the landlord for looking after the grouse moor.'

The Bainbridges were ideally suited to each other and to Birkdale, and they now recall their early years there with nostalgia. The children were young, the problems of schooling lay in the future, and they were able to rear a good stock of sheep and cattle. Mary thrived in conditions which would have destroyed most women; hauling water from the beck, looking after the cattle when Brian was shepherding on the high pasture and never yearning for shops and neighbours.

'I never did care much for shopping anyway. I prefer to buy my clothes from catalogues. The groceries were delivered once a month to a point about five miles away so I used to take Duke, the horse, and bring them back in panniers strapped to his back. If ever I had to go to Middleton-in-Teesdale, I'd ride the horse the seven miles to Langdon Beck and then catch the bus. I had to be careful to get there in time, mind, because there was only one bus a week. Brian and I never went out together in five years, except once when his sister came over to babysit so that we could go to the pictures. We set off to walk to Langdon Beck—we didn't take the horse because we were dressed up—but when we got there the bus had gone. We just had a drink at the pub and walked back.

'It was quiet, I know, but we were never bored. At night we used to read and listen to the radio. I had a craze on China and read lots of books about it; then I read all the books about the wives of Henry VIII. Brian read cowboy books. Really, the nights used to fly by. In those days the children were always in bed by 6.30 p.m. at the latest and then Brian and I often used to play draughts or dominoes for who would make the supper. Sometimes these domino sessions used to go on for ages because neither of us would give in; the loser always demanding another chance to get even. We'd end up both having a big rush round getting the supper. We really had a good time.'

Birkdale was at its most benevolent during the first few years of the Bainbridges' tenancy. Every winter they were given a sharp reminder that it was probably

Early November at Birkdale Farmhouse

still the most perilous farm in England, when the snows cut them off for a couple of weeks and killed a handful of sheep. The difference between Birkdale and the lower farms in Teesdale has always been remarkable. When there is a flurry of snow and a couple of inches down at Langdon Beck, there will be a raging blizzard and five-foot drifts at Birkdale. Once they had to have fodder dropped to them by air, but their losses were not serious.

Nevertheless they did know that the storms which rage around Birkdale can be a positive menace to life. In the nineteenth century two men died in the snow, and during one of his early winters at Birkdale, Brian Bainbridge came close to becoming the third.

In November 1836 two shepherds, John Allison and William Ritson, were caught in drifts between Langdon Beck and Cowgreen. The next day Allison was found dead, lying under the snow by a wall. In 1862 Ralph Rumney lost his way in a snowstorm and also perished.

Brian was returning home alone one evening when a blizzard swept down. It became so fierce that every landmark was blotted out and he completely lost his bearings. He knew about Allison and Rumney, and he knew it was dangerous to press on because there are many deep holes and pools in the area. But he had to keep moving and ward off the feeling of drowsiness which would prove fatal if he yielded to it and slept. So all through the night he walked up and down along a few safe yards, retracing his steps a thousand times. When dawn came he slowly began making his way home. It was only about four miles, but it proved an agonising journey through treacherous country Unbelievably it took until 8.30 p.m. Brian had found the stamina to stay on his feet in Arctic conditions for more than twenty-four hours. When he finally staggered into his house he felt more dead than alive and was unable to take solids for days because his lips and the inside of his mouth were severely frostbitten.

By 1955 Brian was seeking to expand. 'We'd been saving up and I wanted to sharpen up the flock, you know, start breeding a bit faster. So we spent a lot on some gimmer hogs, which are young female sheep. I remember we'd saved £52, which doesn't sound much now but it was a lot to us then. Just afterwards, we got our first big storm and we lost 100 sheep, including every one of those gimmer hogs. It was a real blow.'

The storm of 1955 was the prelude to an amazing catalogue of hardship which the Bainbridges and their children—there were four after Alison arrived in 1957—endured from then until they gave in and left in 1968. First, there was a running battle with the Westmorland education authorities about transport for the eldest, Jacqueline, who, at the age of five, had to walk four miles to the nearest point a car could reach. Mary lost her patience when she was told that Jacqueline's walk would have to be extended to seven miles because the present arrangement was uneconomical, so she invited the education office to send someone to come over and walk with her. Whilst the argument raged, Jacqueline did not go to school for six months. The situation was confused because Birkdale farmhouse lies just in Westmorland, but the children went to school in Durham.

The Bainbridges won their fight and the car began picking up at the original point again, but eventually the only practical course was for Jacqueline to stay with her grandmother during the week and return home at weekends. A year later she was joined by Sandra. Even when the landlord of Birkdale—with whom the Bainbridges enjoy a happy relationship—paid £3,000 in 1960 to put a road within a mile and a half of the farm, there was still trouble over school transport. Mary was furious when she was asked at one meeting 'Why do you live at a place like that?' 'It was as though we were committing a crime living out here. Anyway, it didn't worry the kids. They just loved Birkdale. I never saw them all day because they used to run out on the hills, building little houses with stones, playing around the beck and riding the horses. They made up for the gaps in their education by working hard and Jacqueline won a place at Appleby Grammar School.

'Apart from Tommy we had no real health worries. In fact we only called the doctor once in seventeen years, and that was when Tommy pushed a stick down his throat and only just missed lockjaw. I never bothered to call him for the usual ailments like measles,

34

Jacqueline with Sandra, Alison and Tommy in front

mumps, chicken-pox and whooping-cough. Mind you, I caught them along with the children because I'd never had them myself, but I managed without any doctor.

'It was traditional for folks living at Birkdale not to bother the doctor unless there was something seriously wrong. They tell a story about a man called Ned Mason who lived here for twenty-two years and used to do a bit of gamekeeping. One day about forty-five years ago he was cleaning one of the guns after a shoot and obviously forgot to check to see if it was loaded. He had his thumb over both barrels and was rubbing it down when he touched the triggers and let both cartridges off. His thumb was blown clean off—you can still see the marks of the pellets in the ceiling—but old Ned didn't bother about a doctor. He just bound up the stump and carried on.

'But our Tommy was a problem from the day he was born. To begin with he had trouble with his eyes, which were crossed. And on the day we arrived at Birkdale I noticed something else wrong with him. It turned out

35

to be a double hernia. I went with him into hospital at
Newcastle for the operation and I'll never forget what
happened when the ambulance brought us back. It got
as far as it could but there were still another four miles
to go. The ambulance man said he was obliged to
deliver us to the door and began to carry Tommy the
rest of the way. Then it came on to snow and I had to
take over. We had to shelter behind walls when the
blizzard came on really bad. The poor man, he was in a
real state.

'Tommy had to go into hospital for operations on his
eyes, too, but the worst time came when he was five and
the school medical revealed a heart murmur. I had to go
to Newcastle again to see a specialist who said he had a
hole in his heart. It was a real shock. You see, I'd been
hard on him because he was the only boy and he'd
seemed a bit fat and lazy. The specialist said we could
do one of two things: take a gamble and let him have
the operation, which was a fifty-fifty chance; or let him
go on as he was, which would have meant him slowly
becoming a cripple and dying at around fourteen. He
told us we had a year in which to make up our minds.
That year was the hardest of them all. I'd hate to live
through it again. Anyway, we decided to risk the
operation. (There really wasn't a choice, was there?) I
went into hospital with him and thankfully it was a
complete success. Tommy is twenty-one now and to
look at him you'd think nothing had ever ailed him.
He's a big, strapping lad working down Lunedale mine
on the road to Brough. But once Brian and me tried to
count how many times he'd been into hospital for
operations and check-ups and we could remember
thirty-five occasions. And most times we had to carry
him down to Langdon Beck.'

After that it seemed that the Bainbridges were going
to be able to cope with anything Birkdale could throw
at them. Water had been piped into the house in 1956
and a year later a back boiler was installed to give them
the luxury of constant hot water. They were also able
to afford a Land Rover. Brian learned how to resist the
winters, keeping his stock losses down to a reasonable
average of twenty a year, while Mary developed a
system to beat food shortages during the weeks they

36

were cut-off. She would stock up with emergency rations in September: 25lb. of sugar; 12lb. each of butter, margarine and lard; 4 stone of plain flour and boxes full of tinned foods.

Then came the storm of 1963. It began on 27th December with a quiet but steady snowfall. Brian had gone down to Middleton-in-Teesdale for a pigeon shoot and to pick up forty gallons of diesel fuel for the generator which had just been installed in the barn. There was to have been a real celebration on his return: the switching on of Birkdale's first electric light.

'Unfortunately I had a few drinks and forgot the diesel fuel. When I got back up to Birkdale the storm was so bad that I thought I'd better get the Land Rover back down to the road so I'd be able to walk out and use it down there if we were snowed in. But the snow came on so quick that I was blocked-in and had to leave it at the front of the house. That was the last time I saw it for months.

'Aye, that was a storm. It lasted right through 'til April, blasting and blowing until the snow came right up to our bedroom window. We used to have to tunnel our way out every morning. It was no use trying to clear it away because it all came back again during the night. I had to take a shovel to bed with me.

'The snow covering the beck was fourteen feet deep so I dug a tunnel down to the water, then led the cattle in one at a time to drink, and backed them out again. That took a fair time every day. Then I had to go out and try to find my sheep. A lot of them were buried under drifts but they can survive like that for up to a fortnight unless a lot get on top of each other. It's not too difficult to find them under the snow because you know roughly where they go to shelter against the winds and my dog Fred is pretty good at smelling them out. Then you dig a hole, haul them up and send 'em off to join the others. At night I used to go out and try to drive them into the best shelter, but another problem cropped up because of the hard frost. It was so cold that their wool used to freeze into the ground during the night and they couldn't get on their feet in the morning.

'In a situation like the one in 1963 you're pretty helpless. I tried to keep the sheep on the move, tried to

37

help them get some feed and then watched as they began to die one by one. At night I'd look at them and see one moving slower than the rest, and I'd know that it would be dead in the morning. There's nothing you can do except just hope it stops, that's all.'

Inside the house, Mary's food stocks began to dwindle because all the children were trapped at Birkdale and unable to go to school for nearly four months. Four healthy appetites which were not being partly satisfied by school dinners.

'Towards the end I got a bit worried. We weren't starving but we didn't have much variation in the meals. The meat had run out and we had been on bread and baked beans for what seemed an awful long time. The meal was running out for the animals in the byre, too, so one day in February Brian decided he would have to try and find a way down to Langdon Beck to get help. It took him all day to get down and he had to spend the night at his mother's place before coming back. But our friends and the Farmers' Union got together and organised an airlift by helicopter. Brian was told to listen to the five-to-one northern news on the radio for a message telling us when the helicopter would land. Sure enough it was broadcast. I'll never forget when it came. It was Sunday 14th February. All the children were sitting on a form by the window eating their tea—beans again—when we heard it. We couldn't see out of the windows, of course. The children got all excited and dashed out shouting that they'd be able to have something different to eat at last. The helicopter pilot said it was an amazing sight as they ran out of the tunnel one by one, just like rabbits popping out of a warren. We had to hold the children back from the blades as they unloaded groceries, and hay and fodder for the animals. They made nine drops that afternoon and the following day. We had one lovely surprise, too. One of Brian's friends had smuggled three five-gallon drums of diesel fuel on board—you weren't supposed to carry it on a helicopter—so we were able to start up the generator for the first time. What a party we had that night, with all that food to eat and the lights blazing away.'

But the celebratory mood did not last for long. Although the sheep now had cake and hay put down

39

for them they clearly were not recovering their normal
vigour, and as lambing time came near they began to
die in ever-increasing numbers. Brian ploughed desper-
ately around the pasture trying to stir life back into his
flock but the relentlessly Arctic temperatures at night
slowly sapped their resistance.

'Funnily enough, it was the fattest that died first.
They were full of cake and hay, but that was something
they had never been used to, and they stopped bother-
ing to go and look for their own food. I had some sheep
way up on the fell that I couldn't get to, and they
survived although they had nothing to eat except what
they could find for themselves by scratching around in
the heather. That way they got exercise, too, you see.
I didn't get many lambs off them, but they lived. The
others died of silent pneumonia, not starvation. It was
just too long a winter for them.'

As the snows slowly melted in April, the carcasses of
sheep appeared all round the fells of Birkdale. The
Bainbridges' own flock of 250 sheep was totally wiped
out and half the landlord's flock of 200 also lay dead.
350 sheep in all, worth £3,000. After more than twelve
unremitting years of back-breaking work and primitive

living, all the Bainbridges had to show for their effort was a debt. They owed the landlord for 100 sheep.

Together Brian and Mary went out on to the fells to bury their dead and salvage what they could of the pitifully small lamb crop. For Mary this was the worst moment of the entire disaster.

'You felt so empty, standing there looking around, with your lambing tackle in your hand, when there weren't any lambs to speak of. It was so quiet. The place was just dead. It was terrible. One of our friends came over to help Brian, and together they dug a big hole to bury the sheep. It was so full that they had to jump up and down on the corpses to get them all in.'

'The only animals to do well out of that storm were the dogs. They were as fat as butter because they'd been eating the dead sheep. As for us, we couldn't touch meat for months after that, particularly mutton.'

After a period of numb despair, the Bainbridges decided to do what they were best at—fighting back. Brian stoically hitched Duke the horse to his Land Rover, hauled it out of the remains of the drift which had completely covered it for months, and started it up again. He drove straight to the bank in Barnard Castle and, with the help of his landlord who stood guarantor, persuaded the manager to advance an overdraft of £1,000. He was ready to start again.

The next two years taxed the Bainbridges' endurance to the limit. In order to pay off the debt quickly, Brian had to go back into mining. He took a day-job at Lunedale mine, between Middleton-in-Teesdale and Brough, which meant that Mary had to cope with all the farm work until he came back at 5 p.m. Then he would toil into the night. The situation was eased a little when Brian landed a foreman's job during the building of Cowgreen reservoir, just over a mile away from Birkdale. Incidentally this reservoir flooded the mine where Brian had worked as a youth.

By 1968 they had recovered financially. The debt was paid, the winters had been comparatively mild and they had built their flock up to the old numbers. But Mary became pregnant.

'It was expecting the baby that really made us decide to leave Birkdale. Mind you, we were worried about

risking everything again because we were due for
another bad winter. We were nicely bred-up and Brian
had this good job at Cowgreen so we handed our notice
in. Not long after that I lost the baby. It happened on a
Monday when Brian was out clipping the sheep and I
was three months gone. I decided to try and do without
the doctor—get over it by myself as usual—and I didn't
tell Brian about it. But by the following Friday I was
really bad and I had to tell him. He drove me through
the night to hospital.

'Then we realised our mistake. It was only because I
didn't think I could face Birkdale with another baby
that made us want to leave. And now the baby was gone.
But the notice had been delivered. When it came to
leaving we were all heartbroken, including the children.
The removal was quite ridiculous because the two men
who came to help us with loading the furniture on to
the trailer arrived a bit tight so we decided to drown
our sorrows, too. When we finally got on our way they
tied some of my underwear to the trailer. We were in
quite a state.'

The Bainbridges had hoped to take over a farm in
Eskdale, Cumberland, but the arrangement fell through
and they had to move to a farm near Appleby where
they lived in a tied cottage. Brian worked as a labourer
on the farm for six months. Mary was more miserable
than she had ever been.

'For the first time in my life I was living next door to
a neighbour and I hated it. Oh, I hated it. I cried every
day. In fact I seemed to be crying all the time.'

Brian looks back on that time of their lives in a more
practical way. 'We were lucky to get out when we did,
you know, because there was a very hard winter
immediately afterwards. The young couple who took
over from us had a bad time and lost a lot of sheep. I
know Mary was pining for Birkdale, but we might have
lost the lot again if we had stayed.

'Anyway, the people who followed us only kept
going long enough to build up their flock again and
then they left, so Birkdale came back on the market.
By that time we'd taken over Knott Hill Farm down on
the road near Langdon Beck, but I decided to hang on
to that for Tommy and take Birkdale for ourselves. The

landlord was pleased to have us back because we always got on so well with him and I was able to tell Mary on her birthday that we were going back to Birkdale. I got away with just a bunch of flowers and the good news that year!'

Now the Bainbridges think they have the measure of Birkdale. There are none of the old worries about the education of the children—Jacqueline and Sandra are married, Tommy is helping to run Knott Hill and Alison is sitting for her O-levels. When the storms come again, they can move children and sheep down to the kinder pastures of Knott Hill.

Brian and Mary are too wise to take Birkdale for granted, however. If they ever needed a sharp reminder about its ferocity, they got one within forty-eight hours of their happy return. A sudden fell storm blotted out the landscape and buried a dozen sheep under six-foot drifts. Down at Langdon Beck there was just a light covering. It interrupted their removal and, once again, Brian found himself scrabbling with Fred, the dog, to find the sheep and drag them out. But the expertise garnered over seventeen years at Birkdale paid off and only one ewe died.

Brian Bainbridge rarely allows himself to reveal much emotion, whatever the pressures, but he trans-mits a deep contentment now as he roams the fells around Birkdale, moving his flock around one of the most spectacular landscapes in Britain with the help of Fred and the two young dogs he has under training.

'I like these hills and I like Swaledale sheep. I like the quiet. You can let yourself rip up here, and there's nobody to bother you. I've always liked it here.'

Mary Bainbridge says it's almost impossible to explain how she feels about Birkdale. 'You'd have to live here to really understand how I feel. I just love it. I just love the hills and the sheep and the loneliness. I don't want to live any other way. If I hadn't got married I would have lived like Hannah Hauxwell—exactly like her.'

Clearly, the Bainbridges are back at Birkdale to stay, whatever happens.

Sons and Daughters of the Vikings

Swaledale is one of the easiest dales to reach, yet it has more feeling of remoteness than any of the other much-visited dales. There is a sense of wild individuality about the place, as though the spirits of the Vikings who came to colonise Swaledale still breathe their uncompromising influence over its dramatically beautiful fells and sinuous river.

The Vikings, who had a real eye for grandeur, were generally very selective about the areas they chose to conquer on a permanent basis. Perhaps they felt a need for their home to complement their image. The Norsemen certainly preferred Swaledale to any of the neighbouring valleys, and left a permanent memorial to their presence in the guttural placenames of Swaledale; like Reeth, Gunnerside, Keld, Muker and the marvellous little village of Crackpot, which is Norse for crow's nest. The violence which was an integral part of the Viking lifestyle also seems to hang in the air of Swaledale. Not that the local people would ever reach for a double-headed axe these days, but they and their

Old Muker

45

CAT HOLE INN, SWALEDALE. 1090 feet above sea level. 11 miles from Kirkby Stephen.

legends clearly have a rough edge. There's more blood spilled in the stories of Swaledale, more pugnacity in the character of its folk heroes.

This latent capacity for violence came to the surface less than twenty years ago in a celebrated incident at the Cat Hole Inn in Keld. A local Methodist lay preacher and his brother, who were both teetotallers, bought the inn and closed it down, turning it into a private dwelling which it remains to this day. The Cat Hole had been the centre of the village's social life for many generations—the local doctor left medicine there for the outlying farms—and to get to the next pub meant a walk of at least four miles. In the newspaper stories of the time, the new owner declared 'I have preached against the evils of drink, but that is not the sole reason. There is my brother and my mother, and we need another house. If the local people want somewhere to meet, there is the village hall and reading room.'

The fury of the people of Keld exploded and they virtually laid siege to the Cat Hole when the two brothers took it over. Stones flew and eight windows were smashed. This anger spread over the Buttertubs Pass into Hawes where the men of Wensleydale were incautious enough to make fun of the situation. One of the tables in the White Hart at Hawes was reduced to matchwood by a robust man of Swaledale.

Resistance to change of any kind is a quality which runs like an iron rib through the body of Swaledale. From Reeth at the bottom of the valley, to Keld in upper Swaledale, the place remains firmly rooted in the first third of this century. Indeed Donald France who,

46

when landlord of the Farmers' Arms in Muker, spent years acquiring a comprehensive knowledge of the dale and its people, maintains that the last remnants of the life and attitudes of even the eighteenth century still survive. Certainly there appears to be a shared resolve among the middle-aged and elderly (who clearly are still running things since many of the young migrate) to maintain the ways of their youth. When the Swaledale farmers come down from their fells in the evenings they go to one of the superbly gaunt old local pubs and sit round the open fire spinning yarns about the old days. They sing intricate songs peculiar to their own valley, and on some particularly festive occasions they perform the Swaledale Dance on a table top in the Farmers' Arms.

In the houses there is still a lot of home baking and home-killed pork or lamb. Swaledale must be the last place in England where the visitor will be offered a lunch of home-made sausages; and delicious they are, too. It seems likely that the old traditions will persist until someone can conclusively prove them inferior to modern methods. For example when a sheep goes 'sturdy' many Swaledale farmers still send for the 'mazzler' rather than the vet. 'Sturdy' is caused by a tapeworm in the head, which makes the sheep stagger around drunkenly and finally die. The mazzler locates by hand the bladder containing the worm; opens up the head with a mazzling iron and extracts the worm with a goose quill. Mazzlers tend to run in families because the mysterious talent of knowing how to find the worm before you cut is often passed from father to son.

Swaledale is so full of character that you need to be an outstanding personality to become celebrated thereabouts. The man who seems to be at the centre of everything: top trombone in the Muker Brass Band; repository of many local songs and legends; and the man who danced the last, momentous Swaledale Dance, is Gurt Bill Up Steps.

Councillor William Alderson, (he has held a seat on Reeth Council for twenty years) is so-called because, he is over six feet tall and because you reach his front door in the hamlet of Angram, near Muker, by climbing a flight of steps. It is an honour to have a nickname in

Gurt Bill

Swaledale because it generally means that you figure in
one of the local legends. Gurt Bill Alderson has more
legends than most to relate, and one of the best concerns
himself and his dog, a border collie called Tim. Tim
died of old age a couple of years ago but he is well
remembered, by numerous visitors as well as by the
residents of Swaledale. To say Tim disliked visitors is
an understatement: he hated them to such a degree that
for over a decade he went a long way towards stunting
the growth of the tourist industry in upper Swaledale.
He would sit at the top of Gurt Bill's steps and menace
any stranger who passed by; reserving a special hatred
for people in plastic macs and kilts. Tim was not
vicious and rarely took a piece out of anybody, but he
scared the living daylights out of countless visitors who
tended to go to other dales after an encounter with Tim.

Tim caused Gurt Bill enormous trouble. Official
complaints were laid with monotonous regularity; the
police would turn up and usually there would be a fair
case to have Tim put down. But Bill fought, pleaded,
paid up and used all his extensive influence to save Tim.
And with good reason. He was returning a favour. Tim
once saved him.

Bill is convinced he would not have survived one
Sunday in August 1958, had it not been for Tim. That
day he had gone with an elderly friend, a Mr Calvert, to
ring the nose of a bull in a pasture about a mile away
from his house.

'They do say you should never ring a bull on a
Sunday,' says Bill, wryly. 'I walked down with Tim,
who was a young dog then, and Mr Calvert, who went
to get the ring ready in a barn. I was to lead the bull in
with a halter. He was a two-year-old shorthorn, quiet
as a lamb—at least I thought he was— and he always
had been up to then. He was frightened to death of the
dog so I sent Tim way up on the pasture and told him to
stay there. I was on my own—the barn was about 600
yards away—but I was used to the bull and I went to
him with a halter. But by 'ell—he just came at me with
his head, sudden like. I managed to grab him by the
horns but he caught me full in the body and threw me
up in the air. I landed on my back on his back—I
remember that. I fell off and I was going to gather

48

meself up onto me knees when he came again and knocked me flying. He kept on at me, knocking me about—over and over down the field. I've no idea how long it went on. Eventually, he got me down towards the wall and I remember thinking "Well now, if he gets me under t'wall then I've 'ad it." '

'And blow me, there I was by the wall, with the bull on top of me pinning me down with 'is knees and going at me with 'is horns. I could see nothing. But I'd just shouted to the dog—just before. Up to then it hadn't occurred to me to call him and he'd stayed where he was told to stay.

'Anyway Tim landed. I couldn't see him but I could feel him going at the bull's hind quarters—biting and nipping away for all he was worth. The bull raised his head and then got off me. I were able to grab a horn with one hand and I jabbed the fingers of my other hand up the bull's nostrils, and pulled meself up. I hung on for grim death and measured me stride to the wall. I spotted a place with a flat bit of stone. I didn't hurry, I know that, because I wanted to be sure of me footing. Tim was still going fast and furious at the bull —diverting his attention—so I let go and flew head first over t'wall.

'There was a tree just near and I made to get up it. But I'd no need because Tim was still at the bull. In fact he was busy chasing him away. I called Tim to me and got on me way. I never felt no pain then. I met Mr Calvert who hadn't realised 'til then what'd happened and he told me to sit down for a bit. I were a proper sight. Half me teeth had been knocked out and I were bleeding all over. Then the pain started to come on and come on, and I sez "Now then, I'd better be going if I mean to get home at all." If I hadn't got going then I would never have made it home, and when I did I could hardly get up the stairs. The wife was out so I just washed off a bit of the blood and got into bed. I was black and blue with horn marks and bruises from the top of me head to me toes. The doctor was sent for but he was away, too. He came over later that night and bound me all up.

'I had three or four broken ribs and a damaged spleen. The doctor said I was a lucky man. I didn't go into hospital or have any X-rays—they didn't bother much with things like that in Swaledale in those days—but I had to stay in bed for three weeks. I had the most pain I ever 'ad in me life. I couldn't stir, couldn't feed meself. Nothing.'

That day Tim got a taste for action which never left him. In addition to tourists, he had a strong dislike of other dogs, tramps, postmen—and policemen. Bill's troubles were endless.

'By gum, but he was a boy to fight was Tim. He weren't too well liked in the dale except by me. But he was a grand, faithful dog and he never left me side. He thought he was t'cock of the north and he'd fight any dog which came wandering hereabouts. Once he got hold, it was a job to get him off. Sometimes I'd have to get hold of his tail and pull him off.

Gurt Bill with Tim as a very old but still frightening dog

50

'I 'ad to watch him with people, too, but he never bit anyone seriously. I remember one time which caused a bit of a fuss. Some hikers wearing capes came by and one of them must've raised his hand to Tim, who grabbed him, pulled his cape off and tore it to pieces. The police came here three or four times about Tim but I always managed to persuade them it were the other feller's fault.

'But he were a gurt dog, strong as a bull 'imself. He 'ad legs as thick as a bull's. You know, one day I ran clean o'er him with the tractor, by mistake. Front and back wheels, straight o'er. He got up and ran like the devil. He disappeared and I thought he'd be dead somewhere so I went to look for him. I shouted and shouted but I couldn't find him and I thought to meself "Poor old Tim lad, he's 'ad it." Anyway I came back to the house to tell the wife and there he was, large as life. He'd come to the door and the wife had let him in. He hadn't ailed a thing—the wife didn't even know he was hurt.'

So the story of Gurt Bill and Tim joined the many legends of Swaledale, complementing another, older story of a partnership between man and dog.

Jim Iveson, known in the dale as Rabbit Pie Jimmy, used to live at the farm opposite Bill Alderson's home in Angram. Bill remembers him from his childhood days. Jim had no wife or regular job but he possessed skills which were in constant demand all over the upper Yorkshire Dales. He had a way with animals and was probably the best mazzler in the area. He was often called in to heal a sick shorthorn and always in demand at lambing time.

His nephew ran the farm in Angram so his responsibilities were light and he liked to go where the action was. He became Lord Rochdale's right-hand man. When his Lordship travelled to Swaledale with his sporting friends for the grouse shooting, Jimmy always prepared the way for a good day's sport, and delivered the lavish lunches they used to eat in the hunting-boxes during that splendid era, half a century ago. Jimmy was also a leading personality in the social activities of the dale. In his day he was the best exponent of the Swaledale Dance and he played in the Keld Brass Band. He was also famous for his fine voice, and was nicknamed

51

Lord Rochdale's shooting party. Rabbit Pie Jimmy is in the centre as Lord Rochdale's right-hand man

Keld Brass Band. Jimmy is seated on the right with a cane

after his favourite song which was called 'Rabbit Pie'.

Jimmy had a collie called Bess. One day they both set out to climb Shunnerfell in Sledale, about five miles from Angram. On his way up, Jimmy sat on a large rock in a stream to watch for fish. Suddenly the rock toppled over, crushing his leg against another rock and trapping him helplessly. There was no one around to help him so he called his dog. He had a piece of paper in his pocket, but no pencil, so he despairingly tied the paper to the dog's collar and tried to send her away. But Bess was loath to leave her master when he was in such obvious trouble and Jimmy's repeated order to return home was ignored for a long time. In fact Jimmy was driven to pelting Bess with stones before she finally loped away. Bess went home and her agitation was noticed by the people of Angram who examined the blank piece of paper and scratched their heads. Darkness fell and Bess was still acting in a peculiar manner so the neighbours lit lanterns and followed Bess over the fell. She led them straight to Jimmy and the men prised away the rock and released him.

Jimmy's leg was crushed to a pulp and he was crippled, but had it not been for his dog, he could have died from loss of blood. The place where this incident occurred has become known as 'Iveson's Trap'.

A postcard commemorates the legend. Jimmy is sitting in the position in which he was trapped. Bess looks on anxiously!
photo : J. W. Braithwaite & Sons

The sons of Swaledale are as colourful a set of men as you are likely to meet in the legends of the Yorkshire Dales; but they are matched, or perhaps even surpassed, by two of the daughters.

They were both called Peacock and were both publicans, although they were not related and apparently had little or nothing to do with each other. The most famous was Susan Peacock, the landlady of Tan Hill, the pub which stands like a beacon on the skyline above Swaledale and is undisputably the highest public house in England, at 1,732 feet above sea level. When Susan and her first husband, Richard Parrington, took over Tan Hill in 1902 it was derelict. It had been built many centuries before, on the desolate road between Reeth and Brough, to serve the packhorse trade and the local mines, which according to records, had been worked since 1296. Tan Hill was—and is—totally isolated.

Susan and her husband took two daughters with them to Tan Hill, and a third, Edna, was born there in 1906. When it was suggested to Susan that she might like to have the baby in less Spartan surroundings, she is supposed to have retorted 'I were tupped at Tan Hill, and I'll lamb at Tan Hill.'

Less than two years after the 'lambing', Susan was widowed and left alone with three small children at Tan Hill. But then she married Michael Peacock who was working the coal-mine a mile down the road, and together they prospered.

The Tan Hill Coal-mine
photo : J. B. Smithson

The packhorses and miners were succeeded by hikers, cyclists and the early motorists. Susan kept a roaring fire in the big open hearth and advertised home-made teas at 9d. and bed and breakfast at 3s. 3d. She soon recognised the value of having the highest pub in England, took photographs of it herself and had them made into postcards to sell to tourists. The fuel for the fire was free. Her husband discovered a seam of coal in the slopes behind Tan Hill, built a little mine—complete with pit props—and opened up a thriving sideline selling good hot coal. It was much favoured by local blacksmiths and farmers, who came to carry it off by horse and cart at 6s. 8d. a ton. During the long coal strike around 1921 Michael was obliged to hire a man to help him cope with the enormous demand.

Susan's three daughters enjoyed their childhood despite the isolation. The large rocks behind the pub made a splendid adventure playground and they enjoyed being fussed by the visitors.

54

Three of Susan Peacock's
postcards

Susan Peacock in her daughters' playhouse

'Oh yes, it was grand at Tan Hill,' says Edna Parrington. 'We used to run around those rocks all day—I still remember the little house we built in one corner. We went to Keld School, four and a half miles away. Often we used to walk but if the weather was bad my stepfather would take us down in the pony and trap. During the week we'd stay in the village and come home at weekends. This was quite common for children like us who lived in remote places.

'Mind you, sometimes we didn't go to school for weeks when we were blocked in during the winter. We had some very bad winters. I can recall 1936 when the drifts were so high that Mother went out with the camera again and had some new postcards made. Our postman, John Rukin, got through to us and he's on one of the postcards. John was a good friend.'

Tan Hill is so exposed and vulnerable to weather that it is usually the first place in the western dales to

More postcards were made during the heavy snows of 1936

56

be cut off when the snows come. At other times the wind can be so strong that people have been forced to crawl on their hands and knees to their vehicles when leaving Tan Hill on a wild night.

The loneliness made it vulnerable in other ways, and Susan Peacock took characteristic action to protect herself and her family against dubious people. She acquired a revolver. Not a neat, feminine revolver, but a six-shooter of the American frontier type. It was kept fully loaded in a handy position just behind the door of the living-quarters. Susan used it at least once . . .

Fifty years ago Swaledale was the haunt of a Dickensian character called Tom Brockbank. He was said to originate from Kirkby Stephen, but in the jargon of the courts (to which he was probably no stranger) Tom was a person of no fixed abode and with no visible means of support. Part of the time he spent indulging in petty crime or terrorising the more nervous local residents into 'donating' some means of support. And yet he loved children and they were not in the least afraid of him.

Old Tom was a constant source of trouble to Susan Peacock because the wildness of Tan Hill suited his style and he was a regular and riotous customer. She turned him out on numerous occasions. One night he grabbed one of her chickens, wrung its neck and took it to the coal-mine a mile away to roast it over the fire which was kept blazing near the entrance. He often spent the night there.

Edna vividly recalls one dramatic night when Tom had been drinking very heavily and her mother was alone with the children.

'Mother eventually told him he'd had enough and he would get no more that day. So he turned nasty and said he would break up all the pictures on the wall. Mother said "Go on, help yourself then" and waited for him to start. She must have been expecting bother because she'd already got the gun hidden under her pinny. Well, when he did start Mother pulled out the gun. You should have seen old Tom skedaddle. Mother chased him outside and fired the gun, but I think she must have aimed at the ground. My, how he ran!

57   'Now, I know Tom Brockbank used to frighten

people but I liked him. He used to sit and tell us children such marvellous stories, and he would show us a miniature Bible he always carried, a real tiny one. He could be really pleasant if he was the right side out. I remember the next time he came in after Mother had fired the gun. Mother faced up to him and said "Now then, Tom Brockbank, which way are you mekking today?" And he replied "Whichever way the wind blows, Missus" and was no trouble at all.'

Susan Peacock, a thin angular woman with hair severely tied back in a bun, had a caustic tongue which helped to make her a national celebrity in 1935. A radio personality who rejoiced in the name of Harry Hopeful —he was eventually succeeded by Wilfred Pickles— made a programme with the leading personalities of Swaledale. Susan upstaged them all. She expressed many forceful opinions and informed the rest of Britain that some of the folk in Swaledale needed 'a reet shaking up'. In those polite days Susan was a revelation. News-

Susan Peacock with Harry Hopeful (centre) and Ben Prior, another Swaledalian, 1935

papers all over the country delightedly picked up the story and ran features about her. John Rukin, the postman, had to haul a much heavier bag for several weeks as the fan mail poured into Tan Hill. The BBC invited her twice more to the studios in Leeds and the publicity established Tan Hill as a major tourist attraction. But only two years after that first broadcast, Susan Peacock was dead. She was 61.

The funeral was the biggest ever seen before the war in upper Swaledale. The cortège was followed by forty

58

cars as it wound down the dale, and hundreds of people failed to get inside the church. One of the men who carried the coffin was John Rukin.

Michael Peacock and Edna, the only unmarried daughter, took over the licence and ran Tan Hill until Michael retired in 1945 when he bought the cottage in Gunnerside where Edna still lives. Before she left the pub, Edna carved a simple memorial to her mother on the rocks she had loved as a child.

The Peacocks never owned Tan Hill. It belonged to a titled family in the Barnard Castle area who eventually sold it in 1952 for £3,000. There have been twelve licencees since the Peacocks and it is now run by a young couple, Mr and Mrs Colin Kellet, who took over as newly weds in April 1971.

The good hot coal still burns in the fireplace at Tan Hill

The good hot coal from the private mine is still fuelling the fire.

For all but two or three years of the time when Susan Peacock was queen of Tan Hill, The Farmers' Arms, seven miles away in the centre of Muker, was run by Nanny Peacock. Nanny may not have been discovered by the BBC but she was just as tough and uncompromising as Susan. She took over The Farmers' Arms from her father in about 1880 and had some very strange ideas about how to run a pub. Anyone who dared to express support for the Radical cause was immediately ousted, she liked her customers to have acquired their thirst through honest toil, and she would never serve alcohol to women.

The very first charabanc ever seen in Muker pulled up outside The Farmers' Arms one day in the 'twenties. The happy trippers piled out and headed for the tap room to place their orders. But Nanny steadfastly refused to serve them, maintaining that because they were only on holiday they didn't need a drink. Then she spotted the driver in his long dust coat, inquired the reason for his strange attire and, on being told, immediately offered to serve him because he was working. On another occasion two men walked the six difficult miles across Buttertubs Pass from Hawes to The Farmers' Arms, and were served pints in the pewter mugs which Nanny used exclusively. One of the men asked for a glass because he didn't like pewter. She took back both pints on the grounds that they couldn't be thirsty if they were going to be so fussy. They had to walk to Gunnerside before their thirst was slaked. Nanny also served nothing but mild beer and it was always an anxious moment when someone asked for bitter.

Donald France outside The Farmers' Arms, 1960

Nanny was perfectly matched in character by her husband, Kit Peacock, the local stone mason who built Muker's splendid vicarage. Donald France, who ran The Farmers' Arms for several years until his retirement in 1970 and who now lives in the cottage next door, heard many stories about Kit from the old-timers.

'Kit was a man of very strong views and a particularly staunch Tory. He would sit by the kitchen door—his chair's still there—and listen to people talking as they drank. If anyone even suggested that anyone in the Liberal party—with one exception—was capable of an honest or virtuous thought or deed he would get up, purposefully open the door and then stand over the offending person and roar "You—OUT!" The one exception was Winston Churchill, a member of the Liberal party at that time.

'Kit built a lot of farm buildings around here, and there was one remarkable incident which happened when he was putting up a barn at Calvert Houses, a hamlet up the dale. He had a mate and a boy on that job and the boy's principal task was to fetch beer in a back can from a pub called the Travellers' Rest. Well, Kit got a bit behind with the work and hired an extra labourer. The boy kept running with his back can between the barn and the pub while the three men kept supping the beer. One day as they worked they noticed that the labourer had vanished. They looked around but could not find him and so assumed he had just walked off without saying anything. They thought nothing of it and worked on until nightfall. A bit later

60

The Farmers' Arms at the time of Nanny and Kit who are on the right

the labourer's wife turned up at the pub to ask where her husband was. He hadn't shown up at home. Kit explained that he had disappeared without explanation. After several hours the man's wife became so worried that the villagers formed a search party and went to look for him. Eventually they found him jammed in the cavity between the walls of the half-built barn. Apparently he had become drunk on the beer, tumbled into the cavity and fallen asleep. He was still sleeping it off when they found him!'

Kit died in 1923 but Nanny survived into her eighties before dying in 1933, four years before her namesake at Tan Hill. She had been born in The Farmers' Arms, had never seen the sea and never travelled in a motor car.

The Farmers' Arms is traditionally a place of laughter, music and song where Rabbit Pie Jimmy Iveson used to dance on the tables, followed by his protégé, Gurt Bill Anderson.

Another local skill that Gurt Bill acquired was the art of water divining with a hazel twig. One night at another local pub he claimed to find water in the beer. The twig was certainly twitching about but, in fact, this

61

Gurt Bill has a confidential word at the local
Right, William Alderson, water diviner
Below, Mr Matthew Edward Stones finds water at Kirkby Stephen
photo: J. W. Braithwaite & Sons

was caused by a stream which flows under the pub. The most celebrated diviner in the upper Yorkshire Dales was unquestionably Matthew Edward Stones, who farmed at Seal Houses in Arkengarthdale. He was amazingly proficient in using his hazel twig to find metal as well as water. His fame spread throughout the country, and when the tomb of Tutankhamun was discovered he was invited, by one of the archaeologists on that expedition, to join them on a search down the Nile Valley for more Egyptian tombs. But Mr Stones declined on the grounds that he was too old and the strain of working in a hot climate might prove too much for his health.

Music and song are important in Swaledale, and two brass bands still prosper side by side in Muker and Reeth. But the musician best remembered in the dale didn't bother much with traditional instruments, although he was always welcome to come to band practice and take over the baton.

His name was Neddy Dick Alderson and you could say that he formed the very first rock band—only he used real rocks! He would fish around for stones in the local streams and fashion them in curious ways until they issued a musical note when tapped with a wooden

Neddy Dick (right)

hammer. He hung them from a wooden frame and people used to come from miles around to hear Neddy Dick play his stones, which, it is said, were musically correct.

Neddy, a Keld man, went on to further prove his individuality by becoming the first farmer in the area to breed Highland cattle. He died more than fifty years ago and his musical stones did not survive him. Apparently a vandal broke into his premises one day and smashed them.

The Farmers' Arms as it is now

63

Stamina is a marked characteristic of the men and women of Swaledale and there is one farm, a mile above Thwaite in upper Swaledale, which stands as a monument to the rugged quality of the local folk. Moor Close Farm is not as remote as Birkdale, where the Bainbridges fight on, but when winter arrives, it closes like a steel trap. In February the rough track which leads part of the way to Moor Close becomes the bed of a hill stream and a tractor is the only vehicle capable of negotiating the last half mile because the farm is built on the lip of a hill, 1,500 feet above sea level.

Swaledale farmers have struggled with Moor Close for at least 400 years and many of the buildings date back to the sixteenth century. One family called Metcalfe battled on there, generation after generation, for three unbroken centuries. Cherry Kearton, a relative of the world-famous pioneer naturalist of the same name, and his wife Isobel, lived there from the time they were married. They managed with none of the aids to modern living that we take for granted. Their generator did not even produce enough power to work a television set, and Isobel had an unusual washing machine which was worked by hand. Cherry often had to carry their daughter on his back to the road in order to get her to school regularly but he never spent a night away from the farm between the time they moved in and the day in 1971 when they moved down to Richmond. Isobel was seriously ill, and they reluctantly had to concede defeat.

So Moor Close won in the end, but Cherry still farms it from Richmond with the help of his brothers who run farms nearby.

Knur and Spell

In a few of the more remote dales and along the high Pennines, summer evenings are occasionally filled with the clang and clamour of strange sports. They are so odd and so different from other traditional English sports that the uninitiated could be forgiven for believing that he has stumbled on some ancient fertility rite.

There are at least two such sports which still survive in Yorkshire, the more complex being 'knur and spell'. Sixty years ago, this game was second only to cricket as the most popular sport in Yorkshire but today it is kept alive by a handful of enthusiasts, most of them elderly. In recent years there has been something of a revival which has been encouraged by Yorkshire Television, and world championships with a first prize of £200 have been sponsored by Webster's Brewery.

Knur and spell vaguely resembles golf in that the idea is to hit the knur—a marble-sized ball made of clay—as far as possible out of the spell (of which there are two varieties), using a stick which has a head measuring two inches by three. A lot of skill is required to hit the knur correctly.

There are probably no more than sixty regular players left today and the most dedicated can be found at the Spring Rock Inn, high on the moors above Elland. The landlord, Jack Driver, has done a great deal to keep the game alive. One of his spells is a superbly engineered piece of equipment dated 1873. It is the kind of spell which was always used half a century ago but is not very popular now because you need split-second timing to hit the knur (or potty), which is placed in a cup on a spring and projected into the air when the spring is released.

Because most players are advanced in years and their eyes and reflexes not quite so good, they prefer to use

Freddie Trueman being taught
the skills of knur and spell

Mr Bill Baker, Managing
Director of Webster's Brewery,
Halifax, presenting the Webster's
Pennine Trophy to Selwyn
Schofield

George Ellis roars

68

An old-timer tests the spring type of spell before his plays

the pin method. This is a gallows type of arrangement where the knur is placed in a loop at the end of a hanging lace. You hit the knur out of the loop instead of trying to catch it in mid-air. If you decide on a 'laiking' match, all your rises (or strikes) are measured with a chain and totalled. If you are 'striking', then the longest one wins.

There is a marvellous mystique and language associated with knur and spell and any player worth a regular 'spell'oil' has his own pin or spell, plus a selection of sticks and heads. The heads are made from a variety of woods, ranging from oak and sycamore to holly and sometimes hornbeam. Weather and humidity are the main factors affecting the choice of the right head.

The players now have some difficulty in replacing equipment but one of the group knows a joiner who can still make the vital stick head, part of which has to be compressed down from a depth of three inches to less than half an inch. A match knur has to weigh exactly half an ounce and be made of pot. Although teams of umpires and spotters are on duty down the meadow during a match, a knur can easily be lost and then the strike cannot be counted. Skulduggery was not unknown back in the palmy days of the game. If your opponent hit one too hard, a friend in the long grass down the meadow could heel it in when no one was looking.

The ripest character among the remarkable indivi-

George in his spell'oil

'Owd Pige'

70

duals at the Spring Rock is 'Owd Pige'—Dan Binns. Watching him prepare for a rise (or strike) at his spell'oil is an awesome sight. He slowly strips down to his shirt sleeves ('Tha's got more coits than an onion, Dan' is the traditional cry at this point) and carefully settles those majestic clogs. In Elland they call them 'Dan's Hush Puppies'. Sixty-four-years-old George Ellis, of Lamb Hill Farm, Greetland, is another rare personality of the sport. George has been playing since he was sixteen and when he 'clouts a good rise' he roars like a lion going for the kill.

'My best ever strike was thirteen chains three yards,' he says. 'But that was in 1937 and the wind was behind me.' George, Dan and their fellow-players talk about some of the great names of the past when a top knur-and-spell player was an honoured man in his community. It appears that the late great Roland Aspinall hit the longest strike of all time—sixteen chains (about 320 yards), on the old Halifax racecourse many years ago.

Knur and spell is scarcely played at all in the Yorkshire Dales these days, although in one or two villages a lesser version of the game, called peggy, still persists. In peggy the players knock a piece of wood into the air and strike it with a type of baseball bat. It's a school-playground version of knur and spell.

Dalesmen appear to prefer quoits, which is still played on a league basis in Eskdale and occasionally in Swaledale. Quoits—or coits as they call it in the dales—is basically hoop-la with muscles. The quoit equates with the hoop. It is made from iron and resembles a sideplate with the bottom knocked out. The object is to ring the hob, a white-painted spike, or get as close to it as possible.

The quoit is bevelled and (if you imagine it as a plate) should it fall upside down it's called a hill. The other way up is a hole. In play, you win the top score of two if you get the quoit hill-up over the hob. One is scored by ringing the hob with the quoit on the hole side or, if there's no ringer, the nearest hill to the hob scores one point. The business of deciding which quoit is nearest to the hob can produce a lengthy conference because quoits often stick on the ground with edges raised towards the top of the hob. That is an advantage

because the top of the hob is the key area. Tape measures or calipers are always used in needle matches.

Eleven yards is the minimum length a pitch can be. In the glorious days of the game, when every pub in the dales had at least one set of quoits, they played to seventeen yards. A quoit weighs several pounds and even trying to spin it eleven yards can sprain an inexperienced wrist. To keep things moving, the game is played with two hobs and each player throws two quoits at a time. It is not usually a team game and the first man to get seven points is the winner.

At the big annual matches they once held in the dales the traditional prize was a copper kettle. Back in the 'thirties a ten-kettle man was feted wherever he went.

72

King of Wensleydale

Wensleydale cheese is the prince of English cheeses; unique in texture and flavour, and quite delicious. What a pity you can't buy it without someone breaking the law . . . .

Cheese called Wensleydale is sold by the ton throughout Britain, but it is not Wensleydale cheese in the true, historic sense. The real Wensleydale died during the last war, murdered by pinstripe power. The authority for this statement comes from Kit Calvert, now seventy and retired from the managing directorship of Wensleydale Creameries, where he made both kinds of Wensleydale cheese for more than thirty years.

The memory of real Wensleydale still stirs emotion in Kit, who is a clay-pipe-smoking dalesman of the old

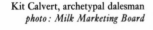
Kit Calvert, archetypal dalesman
photo: Milk Marketing Board

75

school. 'What a cheese it was,' he sighs 'creamy and moist and totally white in colour with an absolutely unique flavour. You couldn't make real Wensleydale in any old place like you can the other cheeses. Not even round here, in fact. Before the war, when farms in Wensleydale came on the market, they were listed as cheese farms or butter farms. A cheese farm had to have grazing pasture over land with a very high chalk content from the limestone. This is what gave Wensleydale that white purity which you don't get from cows grazed on the sandy plain of York or Cheshire. In Wensleydale the cheesemakers had it down to such a fine art that they knew which side of a hill had the most chalk.

'And what a popular cheese it was with the public. Before the war we could hardly make it fast enough sometimes. Although there were 176 Wensleydale farmhouse cheesemakers officially registered with the Milk Marketing Board. Then came the war and cheese had to be rationed. The Ministry of Food sent a man up to grade our cheese, and as soon as he arrived at our dairy he down-graded the whole lot. He said that the moisture content was too high and that there was not enough acidity. We'd have to change it somehow if it was to become a first-grade cheese. But you see, Wensleydale had always been a very moist cheese, with low acidity. It was one of the peculiarities which made it different from any of the others and gave it that wonderful flavour. Still, it was no use arguing and within a week or two we had done what he said. We took the moisture out and put more acid in, making a much harder cheese. We got our output into the first grade instead of the third or fourth but the old quality had disappeared. We had to do it for economic reasons because the price we got for degraded cheese was much lower.

'The cheese made at the farms had to be tested by the same man. You can imagine what the farmer's wife said when the cheese with which she had been winning prizes for years was graded third or fourth. They were proud people, proud of the skill which had been handed down from generation to generation. There was all hell let loose in this dale and eventually they just chucked it, one after the other. They also found out that the 76 regulations said the Milk Marketing Board would have to send tankers to collect their milk if they didn't make it into cheese. That way they made more money because they didn't have to employ labour in the dairy and they got a very fair price for their milk.

'By the time the war ended, only seven of the 176 officially registered Wensleydale cheesemakers were still producing cheese. And those seven were at farms so far away from any road that they couldn't take advantage of the regulations because the farmer was responsible for taking the milk to the nearest highway for collection. By around 1949 or 1950 they had quit as well.

'When rationing finished, the Milk Marketing Board became very worried and said they didn't want to see the end of traditional Wensleydale cheesemaking and so they sent two gentlemen up to me with a list of all the 176. They asked me to go around with them and try to entice the farmers back into making cheese the old way. I told them they were on a wasted journey because of the way the wives had been treated, but I took them round all the same. We visited every one of those 176 farms and we couldn't persuade any of them to start up again. Not one.

'We tried our best to get back to the old ways in our dairy but, you see, we'd been controlled by the Ministry for ten years—from 1939 to 1950—and my cheese-makers had almost forgotten how to do it. And when we did manage to make some in the traditional way we found that our customers had lost knowledge of it too. Shopkeepers used to say "What are you trying to sell us—water?" There was just no getting back. Real Wensleydale cheese died in the early 1940s.'

And so perished a tradition which reached all the way back to the time of the Norman conquest. The Flemish monks of Jervaulx Abbey, a Cistercian Order brought over by the Normans and given estates to farm in the dales, were the first makers of Wensleydale cheese. In those days they used sheep's milk, pains-takingly milking ewes by hand to extract an average daily yield of one pint during the milking season. The shorthorn cow took over from the sheep as the source of milk some time in the seventeenth century, after the dissolution of the monasteries, and cheesemaking became a real industry as dairies were added to every farm where good milk was available.

The farmer's wife had to show real skill to make a fine cheese in the seventeenth and eighteenth centuries. She needed a 'cheese elbow', since there were no thermometers in those days, and she had to test the temperature of the milk with her elbow. In order to start coagulation the milk has to be at precisely the correct temperature when the rennet is added. In those days rennet was made by slaughtering a young calf and curing its stomach in the kitchen rafters. Pieces of the dried stomach, called 'keslop', were boiled and strained and the liquid added to the milk. There was one other way of making rennet if you happened to be without a bit of calf's stomach. A black snail drowned in a bowl of milk would do almost as well.

For many generations cheesemaking in Wensleydale was a summertime occupation which began when the cows were turned out to pasture in May and ended when they returned to the byres in October. The small quantities of milk they yielded during the winter months were usually made into butter.

In those days the cheese had to keep for a long time because most of it was sold only at the autumn cheese fairs. The biggest fair was held at Yarm for three days beginning 18th October. Thousands of cheeses were laid out for inspection on clean straw in the market place and merchants from all over the north came to buy. Christmas was the traditional time for Wensleydale to be eaten in Britain. Quality varied enormously. Some farmers' wives just didn't have a 'cheese elbow' and others were shady enough to use the skim milk left over after the winter buttermaking. This was called 'kirn milk' and made a hard cheese with an inferior flavour.

Until the turn of the century, all Wensleydale cheeses were pickled in brine and matured before eating. Elderly dalesmen still consider pickled Wensleydale to be the best ever made—ripe, pungent and blue-veined. The present dry-salting process was brought to the dales in 1890 and quickly adopted because it is cheaper. However this did not alter the basic characteristics of Wensleydale cheese. In fact nothing really changed until the fateful day when the Ministry of Food sent

78

their man into the dales with his list of regulations drawn up in a Whitehall laboratory. There are no figures of production before the war, but the Ministry records which date from 1941, when a lot of farmhouses had already given up in disgust, give some indication of the devastation wrought on a craft which had survived for many centuries. In 1941 a total of 737 hundred-weights of farmhouse Wensleydale was recorded. By 1946 this had sunk to 109.

Even if Kit Calvert's attempt to resurrect traditional Wensleydale cheese had been successful, the Milk Marketing Board eventually came up with more regulations which would have stopped him. Pasteurisation was introduced and all milk had to be bulked together— good milk, bad milk, milk from chalky ground and milk from sandy ground. Pasteurisation destroys the natural bacteria, thereby turning it into 'dead milk', and then for cheesemaking laboratory bacteria are put back in. You just can't make real Wensleydale that way.

But it *is* still made—illicitly. Real, pure white, crumbly, moist and tangy Wensleydale cheese can still be bought if you whisper in the right ear in isolated dales. It is expensive, but worth it. Keld in Swaledale appears to be the centre of this small underground industry. In one of the local chapels each Harvest Festival, a genuine Wensleydale cheese quietly and anonymously turns up among the turnips and sheaves of corn. Kit Calvert has a good idea of the identity of the illegal cheesemakers but he's not telling. 'They used to come to me, quietly like, and ask if they could buy a bit of rennet. Rennet is essential for cheesemaking and you can't get the right kind easily these days.

'If you're a milk producer, you're legally obliged to give the Milk Marketing Board the lot, but there are various ways of holding it back of course. They could explain the loss of a full churn by claiming that their Johnny was a clumsy lad and had knocked one over. And sometimes they can do it legally by letting some go a bit sour, which is ideal for cheese, but not for liquid consumption, and it would be sent back. Yes, there's half a dozen farms up Swaledale way still making it. Lovely stuff it is, too.'

79   Wensleydale Creameries was the first dairy in the

Hawes Cheese Creamery in 1908, with Mr Edward Chapman, the founder, on the extreme right of the group

Kit and Dolly

Yorkshire Dales to begin making cheese in factory conditions. The firm was founded in 1898 by Edward Chapman, a corn and provision merchant in Hawes who had built up a substantial trade in cheese, buying direct from the farms in upper Wensleydale. Some was of inferior quality but he was forced to take it because he didn't wish to lose the grocery and meal business that went with the cheese. But gradually he talked these farms out of cheesemaking and into selling the milk to him. He reasoned that he could not do worse if he made the cheese himself. The initial daily intake was 200 gallons but it rose swiftly as the new venture paid off. He became a very good cheesemaker and his factory prospered until the 1918 influenza epidemic, which killed his two sons, one of whom was the head cheesemaker. His spirit broken, he sold out to a local farmer who ran it until 1927. In that year, an ex-army captain came to Wensleydale on holiday and liked it so much that he decided to stay. He bought the dairy. Kit Calvert was a small farmer in the area at that time and one of the milk suppliers.

'By 1933 he was in real trouble—the poor fellow didn't know how to handle things. He owed his suppliers about six months' money and then he called us

all together and said he couldn't pay. Instead of
bankrupting the captain we formed a committee of
creditors to run the factory. I was elected onto the
committee and we kept his place going all through the
summer until the Milk Marketing Board came into
being on 5th October that year. We made enough
money to clear all debts and pay ourselves out, and we
gave the captain his factory back, plus £60 we had
left over.

'However by 1935 the captain had got himself into
an even more hopeless mess and the Board had clamped
down on him. Express Dairies offered to take our milk,
but this would have meant the closure of the cheese
factory. Well, I resisted that straight away. In fact I got
up in the market place at Hawes and addressed the local
farmers. I told them that our factory could make a
profit—we'd proved that only eighteen months ago.
They agreed to back me and together we fought the
Board.'

The captain had been very careful to pay his local
bills and Kit and the other farmers found that the sole
creditor was the Milk Marketing Board, which was
owed £4,000. When they inspected the creamery they
were dismayed to find the place jammed with 150 tons
of unsold cheeses. This was probably the largest con-
centration of Wensleydale cheese ever seen, but it
stopped the Board from forcing a liquidation because
there would inevitably have been a slump on the market.
Eventually, they offered the business to Kit and his
committee for nothing, providing they paid off an outstanding mortgage of £500 on the property. They also
wanted to leave the mountains of cheese behind but
Kit refused.

'I told 'em it was cheese that sunk the captain and it
would sink us if we took it.'

Shares were sold locally at £1 each and a capital of
£1,085 was raised. Kit bought a hundred shares for
himself. When he arrived to take over the creamery he
found that the cheese had not been removed and so he
pestered the Board until they sent fleets of lorries to
take it down to the railway sidings at Hawes. Kit never
did get to know where it went until 1937.

81 'Some time before, I had formed an association of

Wensleydale cheesemakers and in the summer of 1937 stocks were getting a bit high. We went to the regional officer of the Board and asked him if he could help us to shift some of it. He told us about a Quaker charity in the Whitehaven area, which would probably take some if we kept the price low. So I went to Whitehaven with another member of the association and found this charity housed in a large mansion. We got on fine with the head man and did a deal for ten tons. But then this man said "Now, when I say ten tons, I mean ten tons." Well, I thought this was a bit much and I told him that if we did a deal for ten tons he'd get exactly that. "That's not always been the case," he replied. When I asked him exactly what he meant, he said "In 1935 I bought twenty tons of Wensleydale cheese from the Milk Marketing Board. One day it started to arrive. It came and it kept coming. I had nowhere to put it except in the rooms of this place. I was sitting here at my desk when someone said that there seemed to be a tremendous lot of cheese coming in. I went into the yard and found fifty or sixty tons out there. The man in charge of the delivery said there were several more wagon loads to come yet, so I telephoned the Board and an official told me there was nothing to worry about: they would only charge for twenty tons, and anything over that would be donated to the charity. And I like a silly fool thought it was a generous gift. It never stopped coming, that cheese. They filled the coach houses, they filled the stables, they filled every available room in this mansion.

' "We just couldn't get rid of it, there was so much. Even the poor and unemployed got sick of it. Then that summer we had a really hot spell. We hadn't realised it should be racked to allow air to circulate and the stuff started to melt. Then it began to smell so badly that I lost all my staff. The fat was running out of the rooms and into the passageway and the yard. I've never seen such a mess in my life. In the end I borrowed some drays and horses and the unemployed miners of Whitehaven came to shift it. They had to take shovels and dig it out because it had all fused into one big rancid mess. It was dreadful work for those miners. But they got it all out eventually, carried it away in the drays and threw it all down a disused shaft. So think on,

82

Mr Calvert. When I say I want ten tons, I mean ten tons!" '

Kit's co-directors at the creamery were hard men. They reduced the head cheesemaker's wage from £2 to 35s. when they took over, and paid the other three employees 25s., 12s. 6d., and 7s. 6d., respectively. Kit himself agreed to wait for his wages until the end of the first year, when the board would give him what the firm could afford. He made them a profit of £1,430—over one hundred per cent return on the capital invested.

Kit was stunned when the board offered to pay him for his work at the rate of one pound a week. 'I'd been paying a man twenty-five shillings a week, plus keep, to look after my farm for me. But I said nowt and took it. At the next meeting, however, I said I wanted £3. Well, they nearly threw a fit and when the next edition of the local paper came out I discovered they had advertised my job.'

Jobs were scarce at the time in Wensleydale and there was a rush to apply. Kit insisted on his right as a director to help select his successor and at the meeting held to interview the short-listed four he announced that he wouldn't be turning up for work the following day. The rest of the board hurriedly backed down and proposed that Kit should have the job at £3 a week. But he refused the offer.

'They all looked at me astounded, and one of them pointed out that it was what I had asked for at the last meeting. But I said "That was t'last meeting. Now it's £4 a week and I take over as managing director." '

Kit's authority at the cheese factory was never challenged again from that day.

After the war, Wensleydale Creameries expanded rapidly and absorbed several other neighbouring dairies. It constructed a large new factory at Kirkby Malzeard. The other dales cheesemakers resisted the offers from the big national companies and looked for leadership from Kit Calvert, 'the King of Wensleydale.' Miss Betsy Mudd, owner of the Aldborough Dairy near Boroughbridge, even directed in her will that, on her death, her cheese business should be offered to Mr Calvert.

Dressed for the Hawes Show

Betsy (right) and Louise Mudd
at the Dairy Show. All the
flowers in the cabinet are made
of butter

Miss Betsy Jane Mudd was probably the last of the great Wensleydale cheesemakers. She was still busily making cheese three days before her death in 1961 at the age of eighty-three. Miss Mudd was born into a family of celebrated buttermakers at Thornthwaite, near Pateley Bridge. Together with her mother and sisters—there were eleven Mudd offspring—she could create amazing decorative displays with butter; fashioning roses and chrysanthemums and other delicate objects, which won many prizes at Dairy Shows in London. At one of these Betsy's mother was presented to Queen Victoria. When she was thirty-three Miss Mudd was hired by Miss Lawson Tancred, daughter of the Squire of Aldborough, who had decided to start a cheesemaking dairy as a hobby. After a while Miss Tancred tired of the enterprise and sold the business for a token sum to Miss Mudd. The dairy is still flourishing in the centre of the lovely village of Aldborough, although cheese is no longer made there. It is run by her great-niece, Mrs Frances Foster, who worked with Miss Mudd for ten years. Mrs Foster says her great-aunt thought only of work and was very secretive about her craft.

'She was engaged three times but she never had time to get married. Work in this dairy often used to start at 4.30 a.m. and carry on until midnight. She used to turn 500 gallons of milk into cheese, every day, but in all the years I worked for her she never let me see at what temperature she added the rennet, although I asked many times. Her secret died with her. She was a very kind person but extremely odd and close about her cheesemaking techniques.

'When she was making a cheese for a show she used to go to all sorts of trouble. The show cheese was never allowed to go near the others and was matured separately in the cellar for three months until covered in a long black, hairy fungus. Then she would brush away the fungus, rebind the cheese and polish it with flour until it looked beautiful. She won many prizes through the years but her greatest triumph came in 1958, the last time she ever competed, when she won the cup for the best cheese at the Royal Dairy Show. We celebrated that night, all right.'

MUDD'S
WENSLEYDALE
CHEESE

Miss Mudd's cheese was sent by post to hundreds of Wensleydale enthusiasts in this country and abroad. Her name is perpetuated by at least one shop in Yorkshire which still sells cheese under the label of 'Mudd's Wensleydale Cheese'.

Kit Calvert also cherishes the memory of Miss Mudd and considers her the finest Wensleydale cheesemaker of his time. He tells a good story about a meeting of the association of seven cheesemakers he set up, of which Miss Mudd was a member.

'The first time the Dairy Show was held at Olympia after the war we all decided to enter. Unigate offered a man and a lorry to take the cheeses down if we would pay the expenses of £8. We agreed to pay £1 each, with the winner to pay the extra pound out of the prize money. Well, after the meeting Miss Mudd goes up to the Unigate man and says "I'd better pay you my dues now because I may not see you for a while afterwards" and gave him £2! Well, we all laughed but by heck, she had the last laugh. She beat the lot of us.'

Kit Calvert is retired now and a rich man. There is a lot of profit in being a good Wensleydale cheesemaker. It is said that Miss Mudd left £48,000. When Kit re-organised the capital of the Wensleydale Creameries in 1944 he offered the shareholders (who had never missed

Miss Betsy Mudd

an annual dividend of between 15 per cent and 40 per cent) £9 12s. 6d. for each £1 share.

'I told them they could either take it out or leave it in but recommended they leave it in. One Hawes woman who had invested £25 in 1935 came to see me three times, she was so worried about what to do. Her husband was trying to persuade her to bring her money out because he'd decided to put his £35—which had grown to £300—into War Loan. Eventually she decided to "take a chance", added £9 to it and made her stake £250. When I was coming up to retirement at sixty-five I decided to sell out to the Milk Marketing Board. They paid just under £500,000 for the company, which wasn't bad when you remember we started with £1,085. And when it came to paying out the shareholders I was very pleased to hand that woman a cheque for £2,700. At the time, the £300 her husband had drawn out was worth around £140. He wasn't pleased.

'My share was £45,000.

'I made certain conditions before I agreed to sell to the Board, though. Some old business connections had to be maintained, and the factory at Hawes, which took 8,000 gallons a day and employed 140 people, was not to be closed in my lifetime.'

When the Milk Marketing Board handed over the £500,000 to Kit, they asked him what he intended to do with his share. He replied 'I'm going to buy a good pony and trap and I'm going to ride around the lanes of these dales.'

So if you see a man bowling along the winding lanes of Wensleydale, reins in his hand and a clay pipe firmly clenched between his teeth, that will be Kit Calvert, enjoying the fruits of a remarkable career.

One in a Hundred

A small army of men changed the face of the Yorkshire Dales between 1780 and 1820. They laboured steadily through the forty years; weaving round the pastures, through the villages and frequently continuing in an unbroken line until they disappeared over the skyline; laying down a geometric design which beguiles the eye to this day.

They were the dry-stone wallers, craftsmen of a high order who built with whatever stone was available locally and without the aid of mortar. More than any-

They create their pattern
photo: C. H. Wood, Bradford

thing else, dry-stone walls give the landscape of the dales its unique character. Standing at the lip of any Yorkshire dale one cannot fail to be mesmerised by the maze of intricate patterns. But they seem pointless. One admires the monumental labour which went into their construction, but wonders if it was just a beautiful waste of effort.

The reasons for this painstaking division of land were both good and bad; but mainly bad for the common folk. In many ways the walls created the working class in the north.

Before the enclosure acts were passed by Parliament around the turn of the eighteenth century, everyone had rights to the common land around the villages. Even the lowliest owned a few sheep and some cattle in the local flocks and herds. This privilege gave him some measure of independence and meant he had to seek a wage for only part of the year. But it was a primitive way of agriculture and as new methods of improving bloodstock and enlarging herds were developed the larger landowners needed extra space to implement their plans.

If they were able to gather together a group which collectively owned one-third of the common land they could apply to Parliament for powers of enclosure. Normally the local squire and two or three of the larger farmers could easily satisfy this requirement. The common folk were allocated their areas, but they were forced to pay a share of the promotion of the Bill, surveyor's fee and other expenses—and wall their land within a given time. If they did not, it was seized and sold or leased to recover expenses. Naturally, few could afford to do this, and the squire and his friends acquired their land cheaply, forcing the poor folk into seeking permanent jobs.

Many of them had the galling task, as wage slaves of the new owner, of walling the fields which had once been theirs. Dry-stone walling became a new trade and millions of tons of limestone and millstone grit were heaved around the dales. The walls were built to a height of between five and six feet, about a yard wide at the bottom tapering to twelve inches at the top. Each

yard weighed about one and a half tons.

Dry-stone walling became a craft—almost an art—as complicated systems of construction were developed to ensure that they stayed up (which most of them have—for 150 years). A fast and skilful worker could make seven yards in a day and receive a wage of around 2s. But there came a time when most of the gigantic pattern across the Pennines was complete, and the majority of the dry-stone wallers gradually had to look for another trade. Over the next century the craft almost died out.

The men who keep alive today the skills of dry-stone walling are few in number. They use exactly the same techniques as the early-nineteenth-century waller. The one startling difference lies in the money they earn. They are probably the highest-paid outdoor artisans in the country and once they have established a reputation can make over £100 a week. But pride in their craft is paramount and at certain agricultural shows each summer they meet in slow and back-breaking combat to decide who is the supreme dry-stone waller. The man who wins Kilnsea Show, held under the shadow of the towering Kilnsea Crag near Kettlewell, is regarded as the champion of England. One man, Tom Varley, claims to be the undefeated champion of Great Britain. Now retired from competition, he owns a farm and caravan park near Gisburn and is worth more than £200,000. No man started out in life with less.

'I was brought up in children's homes in and around Yorkshire and had no idea who my parents were. When I made up fourteen just after the last war, and it was time for me to go out into the world, I was called in and given a lecture. They told me that statistics proved that out of every ten boys who leave children's homes, three end up in prison and another three or four become delinquents. Only one out of every hundred makes good.

'I thought "Right, I'm going for the one in a hundred." They found me a job on a farm on Silsden Moor, near Skipton, at 10s. a week and my keep. I got things worked out right away. A good cow was about £48 and sheep round about £2 10s. each. Plenty of farmers were managing nicely with about twenty cows, thirty sheep and a horse. So I reckoned up that if I could save £1,000 I'd be able to start farming on my own. I hoped to have it by the time I was twenty-five.

At sixteen I moved to another farm for £1 5s. a week and at eighteen I was making £4 a week, but when I reached twenty-five and was earning £6 13s. od., I'd only got just over £500 together. And by then I needed £3,000 to get my own farm. I realised that I was fighting a bit of a losing battle so I took a job as a shepherd at Buckden and spent most of my money furnishing a house because I'd got married.

'But I still wanted to earn some extra money and start saving again. Now I knew how to dry-stone wall— it happened quite by accident really. When I was fifteen and had been working three months for John Foster on Silsden, he went off for the day to market without telling me what to do, which was unusual. The day before, a section of wall had fallen down—about three yards of it—so I thought I'd mend it. I worked all day and just as I was putting the last two or three stones up the whole lot came crashing down again. When Mr Foster arrived back and asked what I'd done that day I told him what had happened. Next day he took me back to the wall and showed me what I'd done wrong. I hadn't taken the wall down completely, you see, and it was a foundation stone which had settled that had caused the trouble. Until that was put right and levelled, the whole wall would shutter right down again every time. Anyway, from then on he taught me how to wall properly and I had plenty of practice next year because it was 1947 and we had that terrible winter. It knocked a lot of wall down did that winter, and we had it all to put up again before lambing time.

'I started to take a pride in it, trying to make each gap I mended look better than the last. I was told how the old-timers walled 100 years ago, and was taught to give a wall plenty of batter, which means tapering it off towards the top so that two-thirds of the weight of the wall lies below the halfway mark. Then to clamp the stones together by following a one-over-two and two-over-one technique, using plenty of through stones which go from back to front, and carefully filling all the gaps with chippings. Coping stones are important, too. They must be good and big to spread the wall properly.

'Then when I was twenty-two I noticed that a Young Farmers' Club was having a dry-stone wall competition

Tom Varley at work

so I entered. Fortunately the judges thought my bit of wall measured up all right and they gave me a badge which said "craftsman". Well, I was right suited by this badge. I was still determined to be that one in a hundred and here I was proving myself. So I began going in for these competitions. Unfortunately at the time I was working on a farm which had no stone walls except one round the garden and I wasn't getting any practice. So after work at night I took that wall down and rebuilt it. But I couldn't keep doing that over and over again so I bought an old motor-cycle and went up the dales odd-jobbing for farmers. They gave me 7s. an hour mending their gaps. Then I started courting Susan, my wife, who was a farmer's daughter, and I used to help with their walls during the weekends. I entered another Young Farmers' Club competition and won it. Well, that started it—in 1953 I decided to have a crack at Kilnsea Show, which all the top professionals enter. At that time there were three men right at the top— Ronnie Eggleston from Bolton Abbey, Ted Ellwood from Milnthorpe and Tom Allen from Darley. Mind you, they were all farmers as well because I don't think there were any full-time professionals then.

'Well, I walled all day and then stood back. There were six of us competing and I'm sure that if there had been a fourth prize I would have won it. But I marvelled at how those three put their walls up. I'd walled my three yards in between Ted Ellwood and Tom Allen and I just couldn't understand how theirs looked so symmetrical, so much better than mine that it looked as though they'd had bricks to wall with. I just couldn't work it out. I had another go next year and came third. Again their walls were squarer than mine with very few double joints—you know, vertical edges running to-

93

gether. But then a judge came up to me and said, "I'm reet sorry, Tom, I wanted to give you first but the other judge wanted to put you nowhere. We nearly had a big argument over it. As it was, we had to call in a referee and he went with the other fellow. But as far as I'm concerned you've put the best wall up today—it'll stay up years and years longer than theirs. For competition you have to do trace walling, and until you start, Tom, you'll never beat these lads."

'Well, trace walling means putting in a stone to look its best, not do its best. I believe that one year a wall that won a competition fell down the next day. The following year I made sure that I trace walled and I beat Tom Allen for second place, which left me with Ted Ellwood to beat. Well, I set my heart on coming out on top. I followed him round all the shows—Sedburgh, Washburn Valley, Fewston, all of 'em—and I stood second to him eight times. It wasn't until the Royal Agricultural Show at Newcastle in 1962 that I managed to beat him for the first time. I took first prize on the third day and the Queen Mother came to watch me.

Tom becomes Britain's champion waller at the Royal Agricultural Show, 1962 *photo: Daily Express*

'I reckoned that winning at the Royal Show, beating Scotsmen as well as Englishmen, made me the champion waller of Britain. I really felt I'd achieved something. Just to show 'em it was no accident, I won Kilnsea Show that year and the year after. There hasn't been a walling competition at the Royal Show since 1962.

'I was still shepherding on Buckden Pike and trying to earn a bit of money in my spare time dry-stone walling because even when I'd been a shepherd for five years I only had £8 13s. od. a week clear, and I still wanted to become a farmer in my own right. One day in 1961 I had to take the wife to the dentist in Grassington. I was told to wait outside and I went to watch three men who were making a right mess of building a wall just by. So I started to show them how to do it properly. Next thing I knew the dentist was standing there watching me—he'd come out to get me to sign a document—and he asked me if I was interested in building a sixty-yard wall round his bungalow. He said he'd had a quotation which seemed very high—£3 a yard. I said it shouldn't be so much and, daft as a brush, said a proper price would be around £1 a yard. He offered me the job straight away.

'I had a week's holiday to come so I took it. Do you know I had that wall up in six days and I earned £55. So I thought to myself "That's more than a month's wage in one week." I started up on my own as a dry-stone

waller, full time. For twelve months I went around farmers' putting up gaps for 10s. a yard and I averaged £15 a week, which still meant I was doing a lot better than shepherding. Then I landed my first big job, a council contract to build a thousand yards of wall going out of Skipton towards Bolton Abbey. It meant I could afford to employ a labourer. More contracts were offered to me and I hired a man who had some experience in walling, and trained him. At the end of four years I had three gangs working for me, three or four to a gang. I got prices up to about £1 8s. a yard and started doing real well.

'By that time I'd introduced new ideas into dry-stone walling, such as using a mechanical digger for the foundations, and working out a team system. I got so well-known that jobs started coming in from far and wide. I remember one job in Staffordshire during the summer, setting a wall back fourteen yards, which meant digging foundations and shifting a lot of stone. We got £1 10s. a yard and started at ten o'clock one morning with a council official giving us the lines to work to. He said he'd call back in a week. When he did come back he refused to believe that five men had done so much. He'd expected to see about thirty yards finished but we'd done 250 in the week with my system for team work. Mind, we worked fifteen hours a day. I got paid £375 for that week out of which the men earned an average of £30 which left me with £255. That's when I really started making money.

'Another week I remember I had £500 for myself. It was hard graft, but the opportunity was there and I took it. I built up the largest specialist firm of its kind in the country. Nothing stopped us working, not even bad weather, which has always been the curse of dry-stone wallers. I made frames, first out of wood and then with scaffolding, which I covered to make shelters like you see on market stalls. They were big enough for a

96

Tom at Todber Park

whole team to work under, fully protected. When they wanted to move on they just picked it up and carried it.

'I suppose you could say I brought dry-stone walling into the twentieth century.'

Tom Varley clearly proved he was one in a hundred. After his triumphs at the Royal Show and Kilnsea for two years in succession he decided not to risk his title and retired as undefeated champion. A little later he had enough money to buy a large farm a couple of miles outside Gisburn, thus realising his cherished ambition. He quickly built up a quality herd and then, ever ready to seize an opportunity, turned a large part of the farm into a thriving caravan site, Todber Park. Alongside the farm is his steam museum, a collection of steam rollers and steam wagons which draw crowds of visitors.

The 1972 steam rally at Todber Park *photo: World's Fair*

Tom Varley (right) with his sons, David and Terence, in front of their three-ton steam wagon after the London–Brighton run
photo: Craven Herald

He organises steam rallies for charity. True to form, when Tom Varley turned to steam as a hobby he acquired, in a remarkably short time, one of the most important collections in the north.

He no longer runs his dry-stone walling firm. The work meant long periods of living in caravans and he decided that his wife and three children should see more of him.

Tom has little hesitation in nominating his successor, a pupil of his called Sam Bainbridge. 'He hasn't got a head for business like me, but he's good,' says Tom. 'I always knew he'd come on strong and last time out he won Kilnsea.'

Sam looks so much like Tom that sometimes he is mistaken for his young brother. A small, muscular man, he was born at Brough—only a few miles away from Hannah's farm—and at sixteen went to join a racing stable at Malton to train as a jockey. At the time he weighed six and a half stone. Two years later he was nine and a half stone so he left to go into farming. That is when he began to be interested in walling. He started by mending gaps, and he joined Tom Varley's team in 1962 when he was nineteen. For a year he laboured at 5s. an hour and was not allowed to build the walls.

'Then one day I walked up to Tom Varley, who was a hard man, and told him that if he weren't going to let me have a bloody do at walling then I was leaving. I said I could do a better job than some of his wallers. Fortunately he is a man who likes plain talking so he let me have a shot at it. I've never stopped walling since.'

Sam's pay immediately rose to 6s. 6d. an hour and eventually to 7s. 3d., often working fourteen hours a day. He became so good that Tom urged him to enter competitions. After a couple of years as one of Tom's top wallers Sam's independent spirit led him to emulate Tom. He left to go and mend gaps for farmers at 10s. a yard, and easily made around £30 a week.

He began to enter shows, and came third at his first attempt at Kilnsea. During the last four years he has entered Kilnsea three times and won each time. He is the current champion.

98   Sam is now moving into the vacuum left by the

retirement of his old boss, although he says he has no wish to become as big. He has two men working for him and another available when required. On good contracts, when everything goes well, Sam can make between £100 and £150 a week for himself. Prices have risen to £2 and £3 a yard. Sam still enjoys gapping for farmers at £1.50p a yard and is so good and fast that he can mend fifteen yards a day on his own. On some jobs he's had to slow down to avoid earning embarrassingly large amounts in a short time. He says there is no trade secret.

'It's something you have or haven't. I've had lads come working for me saying they were wallers but you can tell inside two minutes that they won't make it.'

It was only in 1972 that Sam settled down and began building up a serious business for himself. Until then he had roamed the dales on his own, living rough in his caravan.

'I spent all my money on beer, never saved a penny. I did nowt but drink and argue. I supped fifteen pints a night, every night.'

Then he met a girl, and now he's engaged to be married. Sam is saving his earnings and looking for a house. Before Georgina Cullington came along, Sam's only companion was his dog, Judy, who may well be the most intelligent and engaging dog in the Yorkshire Dales. Sam bought her as the 'wreckling' of a litter six years ago. A small weak bitch pup from a good mother, she had been spurned by farmers who had snapped up the others. Judy is still very small for a border collie but her fame has spread far and wide. She has even appeared on television.

Georgina

'Lots of people have tried to buy her from me. The first one offered £100 when she was just twelve months old. Then one night a man threw down a great wad of notes on a pub table and told me to take what I wanted. But I wouldn't sell her for £1,000.'

Judy has many accomplishments but the most spectacular occurs when Sam is playing darts. After he has thrown all three, Sam nods at Judy who leaps mightily against a wall to project herself across the dartboard. As she flies across it she grabs the darts in her mouth and returns them to Sam. It's a remarkable

Sam with Judy and her pups

sight. Judy can also balance a ball on her nose, throwing it up in the air like a performing seal, and opens a packet of crisps with delicate expertise. But she won't eat the crisps until Sam tells her they are paid for. In the spring of 1973 Judy had her own litter of pups, sired by a champion border collie, and there was quite a stampede of people wanting to buy one.

In every way, it seems, Sam is in a seller's market. His skill as a dry-stone waller is becoming widely known, and should his new responsibilities persuade him to expand, he could build himself a fortune as big as Tom Varley's.

'Semerwater rise, Semerwater sink'

Semerwater is the only lake in the Yorkshire Dales and it looks out of place. It is set in a hollow where three dales meet—Cragdale, Raydale and Bardale—just two miles south-west of Bainbridge in Wensleydale. The dales can present many faces ranging from benign grandeur to a stern and forbidding bleakness, but they rarely turn sinister. Semerwater can send a shiver down the spine even when everything around it is making a pastoral symphony—the sun shining, the birds and the insects counterpointing the clatter of the mowing machines on the surrounding hills, and the Friesians moving gently in the shallows. It seems to be an ill-

photo: C. H. Wood, Bradford

photo: C. H. Wood, Bradford

defined place, swampy around part of its perimeter. The surrounding hills lean away instead of sweeping grandly down and, most important, there is scarcely a tree to embellish its shores. An outcast of a lake, an oversight of nature—which geologists say was formed in the Ice Age because the outlet from the valley was blocked accidentally. Semerwater, although it inspired Turner to a painting, has none of the charm of those other lakes, lying thirty miles or so to the west, and will, indeed, throw a tantrum at the most unexpected times. At the height of summer, squalls come whipping over the edge of Cragdale to darken and thrash the surface, and occasionally dismast a weekend dinghy.

It looks like a place with a sinister past, and according to local legend it has just that. There are many elderly dales people who will tell you that their grandparents believed that an entire village had been submerged by Semerwater.

104

The story says it happened on the day after an angel
in the guise of a beggar came to the village of Semer,
which was built around a stream in a valley. He went
from house to house, asking for food and drink, but
Semer was a mean place and every door was shut in his
face. In the evening he set off in the direction of
Wharfedale and on the hillside made one last call at a
solitary cottage. It was inhabited by an old shepherd
and his wife, who took him in and gave him food and
shelter for the night. Next morning he rose and went to
the door of the shepherd's cottage. As he looked down
on Semer, he cursed it, saying 'Semer water rise, Semer
water sink, and swallow every house save where they
gave me meat and drink.'

The stream running through the village promptly
burst its banks and rose swiftly to within a few feet of
where the beggar stood. There it stopped and settled
into a lake. Every house was covered and everyone in
Semer drowned.

Dick Chapman of Bainbridge remembers people
who claimed that they could hear Semer's church bells
ringing eerily below the surface on stormy Sunday
evenings, and could see underwater reflections of
houses, when the water was still and clear. It captured
his imagination so strongly that when he was sixteen,
just before the First World War, he and a friend
borrowed a boat and set out to prove the legend.

'We camped by the side of Semerwater for a week,
and spent the entire time jumping over the side of the
boat clutching heavy stones to take us to the bottom.
By going backwards and forwards we covered the whole
bed of the lake but we found no trace of a submerged
village. However we did establish that Semerwater was
a shallow lake, reaching a depth of no more than twenty
feet.'

The two youngsters went away believing that the
houses people thought they could see were reflections of
houses on the hillsides, and attributed the church bells
to fevered imaginations.

Then, in 1935, the North Riding County Council
decided to deepen the outlet of Semerwater because it
was feared that a storm might cause a genuine twentieth-
century flood. The lake reduced considerably in size

and revealed hundreds of bones in the peripheral mud. This probably did more to strengthen the legend than all the stories of muffled church bells.

Dick Chapman, then a master at a local school, was one of the first to start recovering and examining the bones.

'We found thousands upon thousands of them and some had clearly been used as implements. Others had been split, not chewed by dogs or other animals, but deliberately split to get at the marrow. We sent these off to Newcastle for analysis, and it was proved they were the bones of wild boar, red deer and Bos Primigenius, a species of wild cattle which died out during the Bronze Age.

'Then we discovered quite a number of flint heads, scrapers and spear heads—some of them were in piles which had disintegrated on contact with the air. Further examination revealed that there had been an artificial island built from flat stones in the middle of the lake, with a causeway leading to the bank. There was a gap left between the causeway and the bank so that logs could be laid across during the day and taken up at night for safety. No marauding tribes or animals would be able to surprise them. There were traces of enclosed areas, probably used for animals.

Dick Chapman with his Bronze-Age spearhead

'There was clear evidence to suggest that the people who lived on this island had left in a hurry: I found a bronze spearhead which I still have today and which was estimated to be about 2,600 years old. It would have been the owner's most precious possession so there must have been a very good reason for him to abandon it.

'Obviously, there had been a flood—a sudden deluge which sent water rushing into the lake. The island hadn't been built very high so the inhabitants must have been forced to flee at a moment's notice.'

So the legend of Semerwater was proved to have one essential nugget of truth buried beneath the layers of angry angels and ghostly bells. A community *had* been wiped out by a sudden flood and the story had been passed by word of mouth from generation to generation in an astonishing chain which began at the dawn of civilisation and spanned twenty-six centuries.

There is another legend which adds to the sinister image of Semerwater. By one bank lies the Carlow Stone, a six-foot-high rock which is supposed to have been hurled by a giant who was conducting an early kind of artillery battle with the devil. He was standing on Cragdale, and the devil was on the top of Addleborough, one of the large hills overlooking the lake. The Carlow slipped from the giant's hand and fell where it lies now. The devil reached for an even bigger rock but he, too, overestimated his strength and it began to slip from his grasp. He made a desperate effort to hold on and his talons tore great marks in the rock.

The Carlow Stone

107

Sure enough, a few hundred yards away on the Addleborough side of Semerwater lies an enormous rock, with five gouges each two feet deep.

The legends of Semerwater have inspired several poems, the most popular of which is 'Deep Asleep' by William Watson. This one by Glynne Ivor Hughes of Leicester, has never been published before, but it is probably the closest to the story told by the dalesmen.

The Lost Village of Semer

Away from the wolves, away from the boar,
    Far out in the lake they built,
Where the piles would knock on the limestone rock
    Deep under the glacial silt;
And they joined the piles with primeval trees,
    Criss-crossed with the swathes of straws,
And their walls were turves and their roofs were ling,
And they had no fear what the night would bring,
    When watch-fires guarded the doors.

They hunted the deer with a flint-tipped spear –
    The fish that fed in the stream –
And their bows were bent and their shafts were spent
    On shores where the wild-fowl teem.
The village of Semer was rough and tough
    And never a King's fair court,
But for many a year it served them where,
Through the summer's hope and the winter's care,
    Men lived as survival taught.

Yet many a time the tale has been told
    Of the saint who begged in vain
And who cursed the village and all it held
    And vowed it should not remain:
He was footsore, weary, hungered, athirst,
    Till a herdsman's hut he spied,
Where they gave him food and they gave him ale
And he bade them flee to the higher dale
    Before the avenging tide.

For that night the clouds crept down on the crag;
   The lake rose up in the gloom;
The sinners asleep were drowned in the deep
   And washed to a watery doom.
Then the piles soon rotted and fell apart;
   The floods rolled over the dead;
Till the grey-goose landed upon the waves
And the fishes swam through the architraves
   That sank in the lakeshore bed.

So, though there is nothing you can see,
   From this legend you will know
How the devil laughed when he claimed his own,
As he sat in glee on the Carlow Stone,
   Where his burning footprints show.
You will find no ruin of tower or bower;
   No church-bell tolls in the swell;
But the curlew's sob and the peewit's cry,
The shadows that pass and the winds that sigh
   Speak Semer's long farewell.

The Forest Horn

At nine o'clock every night between Holyroode and Shrovetide (27th September and Shrove Tuesday), a mournful sound booms slowly across the village green of Bainbridge and echoes around the surrounding fells of Wensleydale. The Forest Horn is calling lost travellers to safety and succour, a tradition which legend says has been maintained since Bainbridge was created out of a forest clearing in the twelfth century.

The elderly man who blows it is Jamie's Jack Metcalfe, for legend also says that it must be a Metcalfe who sounds the Forest Horn. Jamie's Jack took over when his father died; his father took over when his grandfather died; and so on in an unbroken chain which reaches back for longer than anyone can remember. Only a Metcalfe is supposed to have the ability to hit top C on the horn and carry its banshee wail for three miles. Sadly, Jamie's Jack has no son to whom he can pass responsibility, and his nephews are not enthusiastic, so the tradition may die with him.

At least one authority on local matters disputes that the horn was blown to help people lost in the forest. He says that it is unlikely the Verdurers, who built Bainbridge as a place from which to administer the forest laws, would want strangers arriving during the night. He thinks it is more likely that it was a curfew horn, or a warning to the local monks who had grazing rights round Bainbridge, to take their cattle back across the river to the abbey that once stood nearby. Whatever the reason for its existence, the Forest Horn charms a lot of visitors to Bainbridge, and Jamie's Jack is regularly plied with pints as he tells them the story in the Rose and Crown.

And why is he called Jamie's Jack? Well, it is not just to add a little local colour—it is merely to avoid

confusion. There is such a multiplicity of Metcalfes
around Wensleydale that double-barrelled Christian
names are essential. Jamie's Jack Metcalf is Jack, the
son of James Metcalfe. Billy's Jim Metcalfe is James the
son of William Metcalfe, etc. There are so many
Metcalfes on the electoral roll that they create night-

mares for Returning Officers at elections. But the Metcalfes are not just a large family, more a dales dynasty. They practically ruled the area for three centuries, a fierce, rumbustious family who fought the last private war in England.

Wensleydale Metcalfes were paying taxes (no doubt reluctantly) to Edward III in 1300 but the real empire builder was James Metcalfe of Worton, who went to fight in the French campaign of 1415 with his master, Sir Richard Scrope of Bolton Castle. It is likely that Shakespeare based his unfortunate character Lord Scroop of Masham in *Henry V* on Sir Richard Scrope. He had him executed for treason, which gave rise to the expression 'hanging a Scroop'.

By the time Henry V came to speak those immortal words before Agincourt, crafty James Metcalfe had become quartermaster to Sir Richard and set himself up as a dealer in booty. The common soldiers would come to him with the hardware they had looted along the way and he would give them the money they needed for drinks and women. Somehow he managed to get the goods back to England to be sold at an enormous profit. By the time James Metcalfe came back home he was a wealthy man. He also had Sir Richard in his debt. Sir Richard had found it difficult to pay his troops over the long campaign and had been forced to borrow from his quartermaster. When the two arrived back in Wensleydale, Sir Richard was obliged to give James the Manor of Nappa in settlement. James promptly built Nappa Hall and established himself as a gentleman of substance. He had gone to France as little more than a farm lad.

James never lost his acquisitive habits and rapidly added more land and farms to his estates, tenanting most of them with relatives. He built Raydale House, near Semerwater, and became Chief Forester of Wensleydale, the first of many honours the Metcalfes collected down the years. They were also prodigiously prolific. When Sir Christopher Metcalfe became High Sheriff of York in 1555 he rode into York to take up his appointment at the head of 300 men, every one a Metcalfe, and each seated on a white horse.

113   If there was one thing the Metcalfes liked better than

increasing their lands and progeny, it was fighting. They galloped eagerly to join in every battle fought in those bloodthirsty days, and were particularly prominent on the field of Flodden. They fought with the Yorkists during the Wars of the Roses and typically managed to avoid punishment when Lancaster finally won, although many other Yorkshire families were stripped of land and heavily fined. The Metcalfes developed a remarkable system of self protection, for whenever one of them became embroiled with the law and was in danger of losing his lands he would quickly sell to another Metcalfe for a shilling. The property would be returned when all was well again. When all else failed, they resorted to bribery and at least two Metcalfes were saved from the gallows by large sums discreetly placed in the right pockets.

A century after James returned from France, the Metcalfes controlled practically the whole of Wensleydale and their power seemed inviolate. But, as so often happens in families of this kind, a wastrel came along. It was the same Sir Christopher Metcalfe who made that spectacular gesture in York. He developed ostentation to a degree unheard of in Wensleydale, living so grandly that his estates had to be sold, one by one. It is said he entertained Mary, Queen of Scots, at Nappa Hall during her imprisonment at Bolton Castle. By the time his infant son, Sir Thomas, inherited, there was not much left of real importance—just Nappa Hall and the Raydale estate.

A kinsman looked after the affairs of the young Sir Thomas and apparently mismanaged them—maybe even took some of the land for himself. When Sir Thomas came of age and took over his estates he became very angry indeed. He discovered that pieces of his land in the Pateley Bridge area had mysteriously passed into other hands. True to family form, he sounded a clarion call and rode furiously into battle at the head of a regiment of Metcalfes to claim back his possessions.

But he was unable to repair the damage wrought by his father. By 1610 he was so pressed for funds that he mortgaged Raydale House for £1,000 to a William Robinson, an ambitious man from Worton, where they must specialise in entrepreneurs since James, the founder of the Metcalfe fortune hailed from there. Sir Thomas was to remain in possession of the property but had to pay Robinson an annual rent of £100 and then redeem the mortgage for £1,000 at the end of six years. But Sir Thomas did not pay either rent or capital, and William Robinson had to go to court to get possession. He was successful and his son, John, moved into Raydale. However he was not allowed to remain there for long. Within a month he had been thrown out by the redoubtable Sir Thomas, a man of such swarthy countenance that he was dubbed the 'Black Knight of Nappa'.

Robinson invoked the law again and brought a successful action for trespass at York Assizes in July 1616. But the Metcalfe influence was still so strong locally that it was May 1617 before the officers of the law finally summoned up the courage to implement the court's decision and give Raydale back to the Robinsons.

Sir Thomas promptly stormed round the dale, collecting his forces and declaring that he would 'recover by club law what I have been deprived of by common law.' He led sixty Metcalfes and followers up to Raydale and laid siege to the house in the last private war recorded in this country. They were armed with muskets, pikes, javelins and long bows and gave Raydale a preliminary peppering before demanding surrender. The Robinsons refused and the siege began in earnest. A lively account of the battle contained in the minutes of Star Chamber says that the Metcalfes fired their muskets into the house seventeen times during the first hour. John Robinson sent his mother for help but she was caught fleeing from the house in her stockinged feet and attacked. Mrs Robinson was left for dead in a ditch but she recovered and found a horse. She rode to a retired general called Dakin, who was also a justice of the peace in Wensleydale, and appealed to him. But he was loath to take on the Black Knight when the rage was upon him and sent a message to the authorities in York.

That took time, of course, and the siege of Raydale went on for three days. The Metcalfe women came to urge their men forward and Lady Metcalfe even tried to bribe one of the women to set fire to the house.

But Raydale House had been built by the Metcalfes in a superb, defensive position against the Scots who used to raid down as far as Wensleydale, and it proved a difficult place to storm. The Robinsons, aided by a family called Dent, stubbornly held out against the crude weapons of the day. In fact the only casualty of three days' steady fighting was sustained by the Metcalfe side. One of their followers, a man called Hodson, was slain by a shot from the house. Oddly enough, this caused much rejoicing among the Metcalfes because they believed that all within the house would now be hanged for murder.

A company of troopers arrived from York on the afternoon of the third day, and Sir Thomas was forced to withdraw. He went straight to the local coroner, who was called Bell, and 'persuaded' him to bring in a verdict of murder against all the Robinsons and Dents. The jury was hand-picked by Sir Thomas. But the Robinsons quickly took the case to Star Chamber and Sir Thomas was heavily fined and outlawed. He disappeared and William Robinson was empowered to collect the money by selling Sir Thomas's cattle and estates. But he didn't move quickly enough. When he came to round up the cattle he found they belonged to another Metcalfe. So did the land. Sir Thomas had sold everything to two cousins for 5s.

Eventually he went to the Tower but retained enough influence to fight on against the Robinsons and somehow managed to get them into trouble in a long series of law suits. Less than four years after the siege of Raydale he had talked his way into a full pardon. He was also excused the fines.

However he never regained Raydale and the expensive litigation forced him to mortgage Nappa Hall. That must have been a black day for the Black Knight! The Metcalfes never recovered their old glory, but they tried—ye Gods, they tried! As Sir Thomas lived out his old age in melancholy peace at Nappa, his son Scrope leapt into the saddle and tried to restore the Metcalfe fortunes. The Civil War had started, Cavaliers were pitted against Roundheads, and Scrope rode with the King. He was killed when his troop of cavalry was ambushed near Oxford.

Sir Thomas's grandson tried another way—high finance. In 1720 he gathered what was left in the Metcalfe coffers, borrowed more and invested in South Sea shares. When that bubble burst, the Metcalfes were finished, and by 1800 Nappa Hall had passed into other hands. The name of the new owner was Robinson! No relation, but galling.

Rivercraft

Most Dalesmen are taught rivercraft before they are big enough to see over their fathers' waders, for the trout and the grayling are rightfully considered part of their natural inheritance. The rivers are an important source of income to the dales, because annually they attract a silent army of fishermen from all parts of the country. You rarely see these men with the other tourists because they rise at dawn and melt quietly away into the morning mist, staying round a remote beck until the fish have completed their dusk feed and all chance of another kill has gone. You will only find them in large shoals in certain pubs at night, sitting beneath glass cases which contain stuffed trout, discussing the supermen who can catch fish with an easy grace, whilst they toil all day over an empty basket.

There are two master fishermen in the dales who are regarded with genuine awe, men who have raised the sport to an art form. Denis Brown, an excavator driver still in his twenties, does not fish at every opportunity. He is a big-game hunter who waits until he hears about the monsters other men cannot catch and then he stalks them for days before going in for the kill. The Reverend Donald Robinson, Methodist minister at Hawes, fishes most days and although he holds no records, he is nominated by men who should know, as the finest fisherman in the Yorkshire Dales.

Don Robinson was born in 1933 in Northumberland, the son of a miner. Until he went into the ministry at the age of twenty-one, he worked in the mines like his father and grandfather before him. His father, however, was no ordinary miner, but T. W. Robinson of the old *Fishing Gazette*. He was a recognised authority on fly fishing whose articles were followed by devotees throughout the country. Because of his reputation, T.

W. Robinson was welcome to fish on the private estates
through which the River Blythe flowed.

'I began to go out with my father when I was five,
riding on the crossbar of his bicycle and carrying his net.
He used to allow me a length of gut and four flies,
which he always tied himself. I had no reel or rod so I'd
have to cut myself a stick and use that. I learnt to cast
with extreme care because once I'd lost my four flies,
that was it. It was no use asking my father for more—
that was his discipline. It certainly taught me how to
stalk fish and play them.

'To catch fish regularly you have to understand them.
To stalk one properly in a beck, for instance, means
crawling around on your belly because fish live on a
dimension of skyline and if they see anything moving in
that dimension they go down fast. So you have to stay
below the skyline, and cast on your hands and knees if
necessary. It's all wrist work, but I enjoy it.

'I'm not boasting, but catching fish comes easy to me
because of my background. In these dales I can catch
as many as I want and don't have to go to the special
protected stretches, because I can pull them out anywhere. I never fish for more than two hours at a time

The Rev. Donald Robinson,
fisherman

Chapman, arms
tretched, in the Rose and
wn, Bainbridge *photo :*
. Wood, Bradford   I2I

but I go pretty regularly because the River Ure is only 300 yards away from my house. Last night I went down for two hours and I brought back eight trout. I caught at least twenty-five but I just selected the best eight and put the others back.

'I don't bother much about the big fish, although I have pulled a three pounder. You see, the big fish eat on the bottom and go more for the worm, only occasionally leaping for a fly. And I much prefer the joy of fly fishing. If there's a big fish there I'll give him his chance but if he doesn't rise quickly, I'm away. I don't approach him the same way as Denis Brown, who concentrates on the record breakers.'

Don Robinson's skill sometimes causes consternation among other anglers fishing the same stretch as him. Once, when he was training for the ministry in Leeds, he went to fish on the Wharfe near Wetherby. He joined ranks of float fishermen who were getting nowhere.

'But I could see shoals of dace feeding away so I put a fly on. This caused some curiosity but in two and a half hours I cleaned off the whole shoal, about fifty, but put them all back because I don't like eating dace. The others never got a bite and I thought they were going to lynch me. On another occasion I noticed eleven grayling rising on the Ure one September morning. I only had two hours to spare so I put a white honey dun fly on and I caught one straight away just as a bread van pulled up on the road overlooking the river. By the time I had the ninth out I suddenly became aware that the van driver was sitting beside me. When I hooked the last one, he said "Well, I've fished with a float all my life but I've never seen anything like that" and went away quite dazed!

'You see, I know fish and have a great respect for them. You have to know what he is thinking. Float a fly downstream to him and nine times out of ten he'll ignore it. A trout is a greedy fish and loves to prey on things that are helpless, so you use that against him. I try to bounce my fly off a rock or a tree so that it lands by his nose. He'll think it's a fly that's just dropped off a tree and he'll go for it. Another fly I use simulates a wounded minnow with blood on its tail.'

Like his father before him, Don Robinson ties all his
own flies, which is an art in itself. His study in Hawes is
a curious place. His minister's desk, covered with Bible
texts and notes for sermons, adjoins a workbench with a
patent fly-tier's vice, tins of hooks of varying sizes and
heaps of feathers, animal fur, bits of wool and brightly
coloured silk thread. Tying a fly looks as intricate as
brain surgery because a good tier can even simulate the
hairs on a bluebottle's leg. Don uses some bizarre

Tying flies in the minister's study

materials and is constantly searching for cat fur, the tufts from behind a hare's ears, badger hairs, moleskins, wing feathers from all manner of birds, hackle feathers from the necks of cocks, and peacock plumes. Fortunately, Kit Calvert of Hawes keeps peacocks and local farmers dump dozens of moles on Don's doorstep. He keeps his own hens—and not just for their eggs.

'What I'm always seeking is a blue Andalusian bantam cock. There aren't too many of them around but they do have them up in Northumberland and Durham. With their feathers you can simulate a blue dun, a fly which is on the water around May. It is a strange slate-blue colour, very hard to get right. There are some people who say that a fish can't distinguish colour. I think they're wrong. If you have a red hackle and they want a black one they just won't touch it.

'You have to get the size right too. The flies themselves are water-bred and they have a cycle which changes every month. They vary in size according to each district and this is something you've got to watch very carefully. There are wet flies which represent the nymph stage when they are hatching out underwater, and you fish downstream with three flies which sink to the bed. But I prefer dry-fly fishing where you stand upstream and float one fly. This simulates the stage when the nymph comes to the top and its wing cases burst. That's when the trout likes to take them, while they're at their most vulnerable.

'When I make a fly I almost try to breathe life into it. I'm like an artist, I suppose, trying to put in something which I know should be there. I study the flies on the local rivers and pick them out to see how their colours vary in the light. That's where the hackle feather comes in, for you have to display it so that the light radiates all round as the sun hits it.

'I introduced the white honey dun fly to this district when I came here five years ago and lots of local anglers are using it now. It's a good fly to start with. I've helped a lot of people to start and I've converted a lot of float fishers to fly, too. You can only fish on the flood with a worm, so they used to put away their rods when the water was low, but with a fly you can fish all the time.'

124

Donald Robinson with his son,
Peter

Denis Brown does not spend nearly as much time on
the river, but he shows the same kind of dedication.
When he was studying entomology at night school he
used to gather all the flies and insects that breed in the
local waters and take them to the lecturer so that he
could learn every detail of their life and habits. Before
he goes for a fish, Denis will spend hours watching and
logging the movements and feeding cycle of the fish he
wants. When trout become very big they turn cannibal
and start to damage a river by killing off the smaller
fish. This creates alarm and much excitement because
there is great honour to be gained by anyone who lands
it quickly before too much damage is done.

There was one monster which virtually ran riot for
an entire year on the Bain, close to the bridge which
crosses into Bainbridge. It lurked in the shadow under
the bridge, emerging in a wild flurry to gobble up
smaller trout by the basketful. It had to be killed, and
many fine anglers came to take up the challenge. A lot
of them caught it but they couldn't kill it. All through
the year, anglers came into the Rose and Crown at
Bainbridge, cursing and holding their shattered tackle.
This fish even snapped lines with a 9lb. breaking strain
because it was as cunning as it was strong. It developed

an extraordinary ability to cartwheel on the surface when hooked, wrapping the line round its body and sometimes taking it under a stone. In similar situations, fishermen have been driven to gunning down such fish, but that's a desperate measure and an admission of defeat. So Denis Brown came along to save the honour of the fishermen of Wensleydale.

'I studied that fish from the middle of May 1964 until the middle of June. I discovered that in low water it was always under the bridge during the day and then it would swim over some shallows and go into a large pool to chase the small fish. They used to jump about all over the place and the big fish used to show itself on the surface. I realised that it had got way past the stage of taking flies so I chose a spinner, a three-inch spoon which looks like a small fish. I went for it on a couple of evenings when the water was low; but I failed. But on 21st June there was a bit of a flood which discoloured the water, so I tried again at midday because I thought that the big trout might be feeding with the flood. It was, and it took the spinner on a 4lb. line. But it fought back, cartwheeling backwards and forwards over a stretch of more than fifty yards. It ran a couple of times between the bridge and the pool. Now I knew I couldn't rush it and I had to be careful not to let it take the line under a rock so it went on and on for ten minutes. But I got it in the end.'

Denis took his prize to be officially weighed at the Rose and Crown, headquarters of the Wensleydale Anglers' Club. On the wall in its glass case was the 3lb. 10oz. trout which had established a local record for Redvers Hopper in 1933. Denis's fish weighed in at 3lb. 14oz. In Bainbridge that's roughly akin to bringing home a gold medal from the Olympic Games, and the event was celebrated with due reverence. Photographs were taken, and the fish was displayed on the bar for three or four days to enable anglers from far and wide to come and gaze at the biggest trout caught by the Wensleydale Club for thirty-one years. Caught, indeed, by a youth of twenty! Then it was taken to the taxidermist and today occupies a place of honour on the wall of the Rose and Crown.

126   Within a year, Denis had killed another trout of

exactly the same weight, proving beyond all doubt that he was the finest big-game hunter ever to cast a line along the waters of the Yorkshire Dales.

'It was in the Bain again and I watched him cruising around the low water. Suddenly I saw him take a piece of silver paper and then blow it out again, so I realised he must be very hungry. I went back home and got some bread and he took it on his first circuit. I was almost ashamed to get him so easily—it was suicide!'

There was another celebration in the Rose and Crown that night, culminating in a grand sweepstake based on the weight and length of the fish. Denis has gone on to land another two giants, of 3lb. 7oz. and 3lb. 8oz., plus several more of around 2lb. 8oz.

Denis is imperturbable even in the most dramatic situations, but once he did get excited when he thought he had a four pounder on his line.

nis Brown with the monster
the Bain

'It was past midnight and I was wet fishing on the Bain with two flies. I got a good strike and, judging by the pull, I thought it must be the biggest one ever. But, you see, what I didn't know at the time was that one hook was in its mouth and it had rolled over and got another in its tail. So it was hauling away from two points. As I was fighting it and making a bit of a noise someone began flashing a torch from the bridge. I was yelling for them to put it out and they were shouting back at me—it was quite ridiculous. It turned out to be the police who thought something strange was going on, with it being that hour. To cap it all, the fish only weighed 2lb. 7oz. but it felt twice as big in the water!'

Denis is now trying to break his own record. In the summer of 1973 he was stalking another fish, which lives on the Ure in a sinister pool called Sunter Dub, so named after a farm labourer who drowned there last century.

'I've been watching him for a bit. Before I go for a fish I spend some time working out what flies populate that particular stretch of river and then I tie my own to match them. From the time they hatch in the morning there can be ten or twelve variations of that fly, ranging in colour from yellow-green, to darker green and brown until by night they're almost red. Now that fish in Sunter Dub, which is a deep pool, moves out in low water to fresher water downstream, so it must be short of oxygen.'

That indicates a big one. Perhaps they'll be holding another sweepstake at the Rose and Crown soon and making room on the wall for an extra glass case.

There are several forbidden rivers in the Yorkshire Dales, guarded as though they run with liquid gold. Their banks are patrolled by gamekeepers and dogs who can spot an intruder at 1,000 yards, and only a privileged few are allowed to stand and cast a fly.

The Swale, the Nid and the Esk are all closely watched in places, but the most fiercely protected is the Wharfe, where the sport is as good as anywhere in the north. Its waters abound with fine trout and grayling. Dick Chapman of Bainbridge, a man so dedicated to fishing that, when he retired from teaching, he became a water bailiff at a stipend of £5 a year, one day pulled forty-four trout from the Wharfe on a narrow stretch by Camhouses. Some of the best reaches are owned and used exclusively by the aristocrats who own large estates along the banks. Others, equally desirable, are owned by clubs where membership is so prized that sportsmen have been known to wait twenty years before being allowed to join. One club refuses to allow any local anglers to join because their special knowledge of conditions gives then an advantage. With real cunning, they hired the finest poacher in the area as the game-keeper.

But there is one river which for some particularly privileged people is the most precious river of all. It is not a forbidden water and a few shillings will buy you a licence to fish it for a day. Nevertheless it is a secret river.

Those who know it care little for trout or grayling. What they seek there is far superior to any white fish. The secret river yields crayfish; large, succulent, fresh-water crayfish exactly like those served at impossible prices in continental restaurants. Some are like baby lobsters, with claws that can cut through your finger bone.

Every summer day thousands of people drive over it without an inkling of the riches scuttling beneath its